Charles W Upham

Memoir of Francis Peabody

President of the Essex Institute

Charles W Upham

Memoir of Francis Peabody
President of the Essex Institute

ISBN/EAN: 9783337397067

Printed in Europe, USA, Canada, Australia, Japan

Cover: Foto ©ninafisch / pixelio.de

More available books at **www.hansebooks.com**

MEMOIR

OF

FRANCIS PEABODY,

PRESIDENT OF THE ESSEX INSTITUTE,

BY

CHARLES W. UPHAM.

SALEM, MASS.
ESSEX INSTITUTE PRESS.
1868.

MEMOIR.

At a meeting of the Essex Institute, Nov. 2, 1867, the honorable duty was assigned to me of preparing a Eulogy on Francis Peabody, then recently deceased. The Body before whom it is to be read, and the topics to be presented, will give to what I am now to offer the form of a Memoir. The details embraced in the life and character of our late President will be found to be the highest Eulogy.

In order that we may do justice to an occasion, in which a distinguished society, like this, renders its tribute to such an example as his, it becomes necessary, in the first place, to detect and bring to view the influences that made them and him what they have been, and brought him into the relation he sustained, as their chosen leader and head. The institution, and the individual, alike are phenomena that demand explanation; and you will permit me, by way of introduction, to illustrate, at some length, the causes that have led to the formation and development of the Essex Institute, and, as a consequence, of such a character as we have met to commemorate.

It may safely be said that an uncommon degree of intellectual activity is noticeable in the people of this place, and of the section of country constituting the county of Essex, from the very beginning. In the review, now to be presented, the limits upon the occasion confine attention mainly to the immediate locality.

The natural effect of the presence of persons of marked impressiveness of mental traits among the first settlers and their associates, is, of course, the primal and general cause to which results, of this sort, are to be traced. The influence of every individual upon those around him, and upon those coming after him, is an absolute force, greater than is imagined or suspected. It cannot be measured, traced, or estimated. Its invisible, unlimited, perpetual momentum constitutes the dread responsibility of human life—the incalculable contribution we are all always making to the aggregate of good or ill, in the condition and progress of the race. This power was brought to bear, in stimulating the intelligence of the community established here, in a remarkable manner, at its earliest period.

Roger Williams and Hugh Peters, more, perhaps, than any others that can be named, were of the kind to set men thinking, to start speculations and enquiries that would call forth the exercise of mental faculties, and of a nature to retain their hold upon the general interest, and be transmitted as a permanent social element. There is evidence that several others of the first settlers here were persons of uncommonly inquisitive minds, addicted to experiments and enterprises, in mining operations, and various forms of mechanical ingenuity. In proof of the prevalence of this feature in the character of the people, after the lapse of several generations, the following circumstance particularly arrests our attention :

About the middle of the last century, a social evening club, designed to promote literature and philosophy, was in existence in Salem, composed of its most eminent,

5

cultivated and intellectual citizens. The following are
understood to have been among its members : Benjamin
Lynde and Nathaniel Ropes, both of the Bench of the
Supreme Court of the Province, the former, as his father
had been, its Chief Justice; William Browne, Judge of
the Superior Court; Andrew Oliver, Judge of the Court
of Common Pleas ; the Rev. William McGilchrist, of the
Episcopal Church; the Rev. Thomas Barnard, of the
First Church ; and Edward Augustus Holyoke, then a
young physician. When it is considered that the entire
population of the whole territory of Salem could hardly
have amounted, at that time, to more than 4,000, it must
be conceded to be proved by these names, to have
embraced an extraordinary proportion of persons of
eminent position and culture.

The result of conversations and discussions, in that
club, is seen to-day in operations within these walls, and
in the formation of such characters as that of him to
whose memory we are to devote the hour. A taste for
literature and knowledge, a zeal in the prosecution of
scientific studies, was imparted to the community, of
which we can distinctly trace the imprints and monuments through all our subsequent history. The first
organized movement towards establishing permanent
institutions, to this effect, was as follows : On the evening of Monday, March 31st, 1760, a meeting was held
at the Tavern House of Mrs. Pratt, for the purpose, as
stated in the notice calling it, of "founding, in the town
of Salem, a handsome Library of valuable books, appre-
hending the same may be of very considerable use and
benefit, under proper regulations." The poster calling the
meeting was signed by the following persons, all, it is
believed, members of the club: Benjamin Pickman,

Ichabod Plaisted, Thomas Barnard, Samuel Curwen, Nathaniel Ropes, Timothy Orne, Ebenezer Putnam, Stephen Higginson, William Pynchon, Edward A. Holyoke, and William Walter. A subscription was started, headed by Benjamin Pickman, of 20 guineas, Timothy Orne, Samuel Curwen and William Walter, of 10 guineas each, and Stephen Higginson, Ebenezer Putnam, Joseph Bowditch, Samuel Barnard, Nathaniel Ropes, E. A. Holyoke, William Pynchon, William Vans, John Nutting, jr., Samuel Barton, jr., William Browne, Joseph Blaney, Richard Derby, Daniel King, Samuel Gardner, Samuel Gardner, jr., Thomas Barnard, Benjamin Pickman, jr., Francis Cabot, Joseph Cabot, William Epes, Andrew Oliver, jr., and Joseph Jeffrey for William Jeffrey, of 5 guineas each. The Rev. Jeremiah Condy, described by Dr. Andrew Eliot as a person "of great candor, learning and ingenuity," a Baptist minister in Boston, being about to visit England, was employed to purchase the books. On their arrival, a meeting of the subscribers was held, May 20th, 1761, of which Benjamin Pickman was moderator, and Nathan Goodell, clerk. The "Social Library" was thus put in operation. The books imported, with those given by members or otherwise procured, amounted to 415 volumes. The Society was incorporated in 1797. It may be regarded as the foundation of all the institutions and agencies, established in this place, for the promotion of a high intellectual culture.

The locality where the Social Library was formed is a matter of curious interest. In a letter addressed to me, Jan. 11th, 1840, the late George Cleveland thus speaks of it: "John Pratt kept what was called, in his day, the 'Great Tavern.' After his decease it was continued to be kept by his widow and daughters, until the death of the last, Abigail, which must have taken place towards the latter part of 1765. The Tavern House stood on the corner of Essex and Court streets, where the brick store now stands. I can very well remember its appearance. It was an old wooden building, with many peaks; and stood out on Essex street as far as the curb stone does now. The estate came finally into the possession of my grandmother Jeffrey, who sold it at auction, in 1791, to Col. Pickman, and Stearns and Waldo; and they immediately covered the premises with the large brick store that now stands there." The estate still remains in possession of the family of one of the purchasers in 1791; and the "large brick store" is known as the Stearns Block. Our venerable fellow citizen, Hardy Phippen, was thirteen years of age when the "Great Tavern" was demolished, and a few days since, pointed out to me the position it occupied, with its dimensions on Essex and Washington streets, and described its appearance. His recollections fully correspond with those of Mr. Cleveland.

The history of the building, thus remembered by Mr. Cleveland and Mr. Phippen, previous to its occupancy by the Pratts, is not without striking and suggestive significance in connection with our subject. John Pratt bought it in September, 1727, of the heirs of Walter Price. Price bought it, Dec. 1st, 1659, of John Orne, of Salem, carpenter, and Frances, his wife, for 150 pounds in cash "already paid," and the deed was recorded, April 25th, 1660. John Orne bought of Charles Gott. The following is a copy of the deed of this purchase.

"29th of December 1652.

Charles Gott of Salem Attornie to m^r Hugh Peters for and in consideration of forty shillings in hand paid hath sold unto John Horne of Salem aforesaid one piece of ground contayning about one quarter of an acre more or lesse nere the meeting howse in Salem one the North side thereof, running along by the high way being the land of m^r Hugh Peters aforesaid. Provided if m^r Peters shall retorne to New England in person and repay the said John all his charges of building or otherwayes bestowed upon the said land that then the said m^r Peters shall have the said land againe as by a writing dated the 28th day of this instant December 1652 apeareth."

It appears by the deed to Price of 1659, that, at that time, there was a dwelling-house on the lot. The language of the deed, just quoted, reserving to Peters the right of reclaiming the property, in the event of his ever returning to America, upon making good to Orne for "all his charges of building, or otherwise bestowed upon the said land," does not necessarily, in itself, prove that there was a house upon it, when Orne purchased, but the general aspect of the transaction leads, I think, to the conclusion that there was. It can hardly be supposed that Mr. Peters would have authorized his attorney to bind him, on the contingency mentioned, in order to recover the property, to pay whatever Orne might spend in erecting buildings, whether they suited him or not. This consideration makes it probable that there was a house on the lot in 1652, and that Peters and his attorney knew what sort of a house it was. The same general reasoning, probably, authorizes the conclusion that the house was built under the direction, if not the personal oversight, of Peters himself. Merely having care of the lot, in the temporary absence of the owner, Gott would not have taken the responsibility of erecting a house upon it, without specific directions, and it is most likely that, if not built before he left the country, Peters would have deferred it until his return. The balance of probabilities seems, therefore, to be against the supposition that the house was erected either during the period when Orne conditionally owned it, or Gott had charge of it. Its size, as particularly described to me by Mr. Phippen, which led to its being called "The Great Tavern," and its architecture of "many peaks," prove that it was of a more commanding, pretentious, and artistic style, than would have been thought of by either of the good deacons, Gott or Orne. Its position also indicates that it was built, at a very early day, before the line of Essex street had been adjusted.

It is well known that Mr. Peters lived, at one time, at the diagonal corner of the crossing of Washington and Essex streets. His house and lot there were sold by his attorney some years after he had gone to England. I think there is evidence that he had also built a house near the corner of Washington and Norman streets. He was a man of indefatigable activity, was always making improvements, and starting enterprises, and it is not strange that he built houses and changed his residence from time to time. It is quite likely that before his mission to the mother country had been suggested, he employed Orne to prepare a residence, more fitted to accommodate him permanently, on his lot where the Stearns Building now is. It may have been finished, and possibly occupied by him, but, not paid for, in consequence of the suddenness of his call to the service of the colony, as one of its agents to look after its interests at London. A settlement of accounts may have been deferred until he returned, which all supposed would be in a short time, an expectation cherished by him to the last. The battle of Worcester, however, which occurred Sept.

3d, 1651, put such a face upon the affairs of the mother country, that it seemed probable Mr. Peters's services would be permanently needed there. Gott was accordingly authorized to settle with Orne, conveying to him, for the small sum of two pounds, the whole property, reserving, however, to Peters the right of repurchasing it, if, notwithstanding the then existing appearances, he should, at any time, come back and claim it. The death of Cromwell in 1658, and the events that quickly followed, showed that the days of the Commonwealth were numbered and finished. As the next year drew to a close it became apparent that the restoration of the monarchy was inevitable, and closely impending. The return of Peters became impossible; arrest, attainder, death and confiscation, were hanging over him and his co-patriots. Orne, perhaps, felt that the conditional clause in his deed, rendered the estate liable, and he was glad, before it was too late, to get rid of it by the sale to Price.

Such are the facts so far as known, and the conjectures which they seem to justify, in reference to "the Great Tavern with many peaks." It is interesting to find that certainly on that spot and within those walls, the first institution for a higher intellectual culture, and the diffusion through this community of a taste for literature and science, was organized in 1760; a spot owned by Hugh Peters, and the structure probably erected, and perhaps occupied, by him. He was as highly educated a person as any among the early emigrants, and a zealous promoter of popular intelligence. He took an active part in bringing our college into operation, and made great, although unavailing, exertions to have it established in Salem. One of the objects of his mission to England was to obtain aid for the interests of education here. In the course of the trial that resulted in his condemnation and execution, addressing the court he said : "I have looked after three things ; one was that there might be sound religion. The second was that learning and laws might be maintained. The third, that the poor might be cared for. And I must confess that I have spent most of my time in these things, to this end and purpose." When, in fine, the great activity of Mr. Peters, during his short residence here, in stimulating the energies and faculties of the colonists, and by innumerable methods starting society in the path of improvement and progress— so as to draw from Winthrop the encomium of "laboring, both publicly and privately, to raise up men to a public frame of spirit"—is taken into view, we appreciate the singular appropriateness of the circumstance that the first organized effort to create "a public frame of spirit," in favor of the collection and diffusion of the means of intellectual and scientific culture directly among the people, took place on his ground, and in what was, not improbably, his house.

It is quite evident that, at the time of the formation of the Social Library, interest in philosophical enquiries was a characteristic of the people here, the effect of pre-existing causes, as well as the efficient cause of subsequent developments. The following instance seems to indicate such a prevalent turn of mind only five years afterwards.

In 1766, a lad of thirteen years of age, born and brought up on a farm in Woburn, with only such advantages of education as a country school district then afforded, was apprenticed to John Appleton, grandfather of Dr. John Appleton, the present Assistant Librarian of the Massachusetts Historical Society. Mr. Appleton's

residence and place of business was on the south side of
Essex street, the lot being occupied, at this time, by Dr.
George Choate. He carried on a retail variety store, in
the style of that day, and was engaged in commercial
pursuits in connection with a general traffic. The young
apprentice, from early childhood, in his humble rural
home, had manifested a taste for mechanical and philosophical amusements, and had delighted in constructing
miniature machines, and in rude attempts at drawing and
modelling. Here he found an atmosphere so congenial
to his original passion that he was stimulated to exercise
and exhibit his genius. His curious and various experiments attracted favorable notice, and won for him an
established reputation, in an appreciating community.
When the repeal of the Stamp-Act, by the British Parliament, had raised an enthusiastic gratification throughout
the colonies, the people of Salem were determined to
celebrate it in a style of extraordinary and unparalleled
brilliancy and impressiveness. It was voted to have a
grand display of fireworks. There were no professional
pyrotechnists here, and perhaps never had been in the
whole country. All, however, knew the mechanical and
chemical propensities and attainments of Mr. Appleton's
apprentice boy, and he was appointed to conduct the
preparations and superintend the exhibition. Some care-
lessness, not to be wondered at, considering the inex-
perience of all concerned, led to a premature explosion,
and he was so seriously injured, that his life was for a
time despaired of, and his health so much affected, as
finally to render his removal to his home in Woburn
necessary. But the bent of his mind had, in the few
years he had lived in Salem, become so fixed that, upon
his recovery, he instantly sought and obtained permission

to attend a course of philosophical lectures, delivered in Harvard College. He walked regularly to and from Cambridge, a distance of nine miles to enjoy the privilege. He was then seventeen years of age. He taught country district schools at Bradford and Wilmington, in Massachusetts, and Concord, New Hampshire. All the while he continued his philosophical pursuits, and attracted increased attention, by novel and successful operations, in mechanics and chemistry. By a singular succession of circumstances, he was drawn to a military career in the service of the mother country. He combined qualities that soon gave him great distinction in that line. His scientific attainments and philosophical enquiries, always directed to practical ends, were found of inestimable importance, in fortification, engineering, armament, equipment, subsistence and all sanitary and economical modes of military administration. Gunpowder, as an explosive agent, had ever been a special and favorite subject of experiment and research, not at all checked by the disaster of his boyhood at Salem. His methodical and observing habits of mind, and disposition to classify all details, gave him facilities in mastering military tactics. And, besides, his personal aspect and address were precisely adapted to command preëminence, in the pomp and pageantry, the parades, evolutions, and blazonry of tented fields and marshalled camps. He united with all that was showy and dazzling the sterner wisdom, itself based upon philosophical principles, that made him famous as a disciplinarian. In the whole range of biography, there is nothing more wonderful than such a product as he presents—raised in rustic life, on a New England farm, and in a Salem retail shop—a most finished and polished gentleman, with a commanding presence, and easy cour-

tesy, seldom approached by those upon whom knightly
or courtly influences have been shed for indefinite generations. His lofty form, noble bearing, sweet and winning
manners, gave to his early manhood a wonderful attractiveness. One of his biographers says: "His grace and
personal advantages were early developed. His stature
of nearly six feet, his erect figure, his finely formed
limbs, his bright blue eyes, his features chiselled in the
Roman mould, and his dark auburn hair, rendered him a
model of manly beauty." We may well believe that he
shone the cynosure of all eyes, at the head of his regiment of dragoons, and that he made a sensation in all
circles in London. In 1779 he was elected into the Royal
Society, and in 1784, received the honors of Knighthood
from the King of Great Britain. Having "introduced a
revision of the military exercise, and effected several
reformations of acknowledged consequence," in that
country, he went to the continent, with a view of offering
his services to Austria, then at war with Turkey. Dr.
Jacob Bigelow, who wrote the memoir of this remarkable
man, read before the American Academy of Arts and
Sciences, from which I have already quoted, says that
"in more than one instance of his life it happened that
his fine manly figure and captivating manners were instru-
mental in deciding his reception among strangers." On
his way to Vienna, he was present at a review of Bavarian
troops. He appeared, as a spectator, on the ground,
mounted and uniformed, according to his rank, as Sir
Benjamin Thompson, a colonel of the British cavalry.
The commander of the troops was a Duke, and soon after,
the King of Bavaria. Attracted by the splendid bearing
and aspect of the stranger he sought his acquaintance,
and impressed with a deep admiration of his qualities and

attainments, made him his aid-de-camp, chamberlain, member of his council of State, and Lieutenant-general of his armies, and afterwards raised him to the dignity of a Count of the Holy Roman empire. It must commend Sir Benjamin Thompson to the good feeling of every true and high-minded man, that while covered with all these honors at the Court of Munich, he did not forget or fail to avow his attachment to, and pride in, his early humble condition and home in New England. In selecting the distinguishing element of his title as a nobleman, he chose the name that had formerly been given, prior to its change to Concord, to the village in New Hampshire, where, when nineteen years of age, he had taught school and been married—Rumford. He led the armies of Bavaria with distinguished success in an important campaign, and reformed the entire military organization and civil administration of that country. The extraordinary results he secured by the application of philosophical principles, in raising the condition of the whole people, in reducing the burdens of government, and particularly in solving the great problem of statesmanship —abolishing pauperism by bringing it into remedial relations with labor—made his name renowned throughout Europe. Monarchs sought his services, and learned societies and scientific academies in all the great cities conferred upon him their honors. He was commissioned ambassador to Great Britain, but was prevented from acting in that capacity. The old feudal doctrine of perpetual allegiance, not much longer to be tolerated among nations professing to recognize the rights of man, was found—he having been born a British subject—to obstruct his reception, in the official capacity of Bavarian Envoy, by the Court at London. But so warm was the welcome extended to him unofficially, by the government and all classes of the people, especially men of science and learning, that he was induced to remain some years in England, during which time he secured the establishment of the Royal Institution of Great Britain, whose charter expresses the great object and end of his labors, through his entire career, from his boyish experiments in Woburn and Salem, to his last productions.

The absolute identity of his language with that employed to express one of the designs of the Essex Institute, and the main object of the Peabody Academy, will not fail to be noticed, "for diffusing the knowledge, and facilitating the general introduction of useful mechanical inventions and improvements ; and for teaching by philosophical lectures and experiments the application of science to the common purposes of life." His last years were spent at a beautiful seat owned by him within a few miles of Paris.

Count Rumford enlarged, in many important particulars, the scientific knowledge of his day, and published a great number of valuable works. He died, August 21st, 1814, in the sixty-second year of his age, and his Eulogy, before the Institute of France, was pronounced by Cuvier. Some years before his death he gave to the Royal Society of Great Britain one thousand pounds, the interest on which was to be distributed, from time to time, as premiums to the authors of the most useful discoveries in light and heat, and at the same time he transmitted the sum of five thousand dollars, to the American Academy of Arts and Sciences, the interest to be devoted, in like manner, to the same ends. In grateful remembrance of the institution which had opened its lecture-room to him when a poor country boy, he bequeathed one thousand dollars annually, with the final reversion of his whole estate, to the University of Cambridge, in the State of Massachusetts, as the foundation of a professorship, "to teach, by regular courses of academical and public lectures, accompanied with proper experiments, the utility of the physical and mathematical sciences, for the improvement of the useful arts, and for the extension of the industry, prosperity, happiness and well being of society." Here, again, I cannot but remark that it would have been impossible to frame language into a more perfect expression of the ends pursued by the Essex Institute and Peabody Academy, and to which the life of our late President was devoted.

It will be conceded, I think, that in respect to such a mind as that of Count Rumford, the period of his residence here was most important. It was the age in which the deepest and most durable impressions are made. His faculties were then in their forming stage, and the direction in which they were afterwards to work decisively determined. It was, indeed, fortunate that his awakening and kindling genius was placed under the influences that . here surrounded it. His subsequent course, surpassing as it does, in many points of view, all that is found in history or fiction, may be largely ascribed to the intellectual energies put in operation by the men who established the old Salem Social Library.

Richard Kirwan, LL. D., of Dublin, was one of the most distinguished philosophers of his period, and is ranked among eminent writers in chemistry, mineralogy, geology, and kindred sciences. In 1781, a vessel, having on board a valuable library belonging to him, was captured by an American private armed ship, and brought into Beverly, to be disposed of as a prize. The collection

3

of books was there sold, as a whole, to an association
of gentlemen of this town and neighborhood, among
whom were the Rev. Manasseh Cutler, LL. D., A. A. S.,
S. P. A., then the minister of the congregation at Ham-
ilton, afterwards a Representative from this State in
Congress, and founder of the State of Ohio, who in the
course of his distinguished life adorned each of the three
learned professions; the Rev. Joseph Willard, LL. D.,
S. P. A., of Beverly, afterwards President of Harvard
College, and first President of the American Academy of
Arts and Sciences; the Rev. Thomas Barnard, D. D.,
A. A. S., of the North Church in Salem; Joshua Fisher,
M. D., A. A. S., of Beverly, the first President of the
Massachusetts Medical Society; the Rev. John Prince, of
the First Church, in Salem; and Edward A. Holyoke,
M. D., of Salem. They made it the foundation of the
Philosophical Library. Justice to the memory of the
enlightened merchants, who owned the vessel, Andrew
and John Cabot brothers, requires it to be recorded, as
a part of the transaction, that they relinquished their
share of prize money for the books, and made such
arrangements with the other parties in interest, that the
whole library came to the association of scholars just
named, at a mere nominal price; and the satisfaction,
with which the affair will ever be regarded, is rendered
complete by the additional fact, that remuneration was
subsequently tendered to Dr. Kirwan, but he declined to
accept it, expressing gratification that the books had fallen
into such hands, and were put to so good a use.

The Social Library and the Philosophical Library were,
after some time, consolidated into the "Salem Athenæum,"
and incorporated, as such, in March, 1810.

The "Essex Historical Society," was incorporated in

1821, and put in operation on the 27th of June of that year.

Such is the history of movements, in an organized form, to give effect to efforts to promote the influence of literature, science, philosophy and history, in this place from 1760 to 1821. It is quite remarkable, that in each stage of the progress a leading part was taken by one man—Dr. Holyoke; he signed the call for the meeting at the house of Mrs. Pratt, and was an original subscriber to the funds then raised to establish the Social Library; he was one of the purchasers of Dr. Kirwan's books, thus coöperating in founding the Philosophical Library; he was the first President of the Salem Athenæum, and also the first President of the Essex Historical Society. The effects of such institutions, and methods of combined action of such men, upon the character of the population in general, may be estimated, in some degree, by considering them in view of the ordinary laws of social influence; but they can only be adequately and fully appreciated by illustrations in detail.

In the earlier portion of this century, when our population was scarcely half of what it now is, and we had barely reached the required constitutional dimensions, but not yet aspired to the dignity, of a city, there were on the list of our inhabitants the names of an extraordinary number of persons, eminent and conspicuous for attainments in science and literature. It is proper to bring them severally before our minds, as we shall thus best appreciate the influences under which the subject of this memoir grew up to manhood.

Edward Augustus Holyoke, LL. D., was President of the Massachusetts Medical Society, and of the American Academy of Arts and Sciences. He added to the learning

and skill that made him, for half a century, The Teacher
of his profession, acquisitions of knowledge in various
other fields, particularly of Natural Science. He kept
up with his times in the several departments of intellectual progress, retaining the effects of an early classical
training, and enjoying to the last a relish for the productions of elegant literature. A professional practice of
unrivalled duration, accompanied by careful observation
and an admirable judgment, made him the great oracle
among physicians, large numbers of whom, from all
quarters, gathered round him, as the guide of their early
studies. Among his pupils were some of the most distinguished medical names of the country; one of them
was the late James Jackson, long the revered head of
his profession, whose eulogist informs us that he took
"his old master, as he always loved to call him, as his
model."* Dr. Jackson had explored the whole ground of
medical science and practice, at home and abroad, and no
man ever more universally enjoyed or deserved the confidence and respect of the community, for discriminating
fairness, and sound judgment; and it is stated by the
highest authority that he expressed himself thus, con-
cerning Dr. Holyoke: "I can only say of his practice,
the longer I have lived, I have thought better and better
of it." The "Ethical Essay," a posthumous publication of
Dr. Holyoke, commenced in his eighty-sixth, but mostly
composed after he had passed his ninetieth year, is a
lasting monument of his christian wisdom, and shows that
he was entitled, preëminently, to the character of a
philosopher, as well as patriarch.

---

* An Introductory Lecture delivered before the medical class of
Harvard University, Nov. 6th, 1867, by Oliver Wendell Holmes, Park-
man Professor of Anatomy and Physiology.

Timothy Pickering, LL. D., S. P. A., adorned the great spheres in which he had moved in our public and national military and civil service, with scholarly tastes, and a purity, exactness, vigor and impressiveness of style that placed him among our best writers. James Madison pronounced the highest encomium upon his State Papers, while at the head of the department at Washington intrusted with the foreign relations of the country, at a critical period of our diplomatic history.

The Rev. John Prince, LL. D., A. A. S., S. P. A., had a world-wide reputation as a scientific mechanician and discoverer, enlarging the domain of Pneumatics and Astronomy with ingenious constructions, the work of his own hands. His diversified attainments in natural philosophy, and general as well as professional literature, were called into the service of learned institutions, and private students throughout the country, and his judgment, skill and taste employed to aid in the selection and importation of standard books, and the most approved philosophical apparatus. Colleges, academies, and libraries, in all parts of the Union, have now in their lecture-rooms and alcoves, the fruits of their correspondence with him; and machines contrived or improved by him, and constructed in his own laboratory, are still regarded as invaluable, in displaying the wonders of the creation, in the laws and growths of nature, or the starry firmament on high. His home was at once a lecture-room and school of philosophy, ever open to contribute to the delight and instruction of neighbors or strangers, in the diversified methods by which the lucernal microscope, magic lantern, telescope, air-pump, electric jar, or other philosophical machines are put to their uses by a skilful hand. It is impossible to estimate the value or the extent of the

service he thus rendered with glad enthusiasm, and unwearied constancy, all his life long, to ever welcome
guests. Many a young mind was thus opened to discern
the value, and inspired to pursue the attainments, of
science and philosophy. The interest so deeply taken in
such subjects, in his early youth, by him whose character
we have met to consider, was gratefully attributed, in a
large measure, to the happy hours he spent in Dr. Prince's
laboratory and library.

Benjamin Lynde Oliver, M. D., A. A. S., was also
a philosophical mechanician, illustrating his favorite
branches of science by machinery of his own construction, operating upon brass or glass. He was a scientific
musician, astronomer and optician; had an exquisite
classical and artistic taste, and was an elegant *belles-
lettres* scholar and writer.

The Rev. William Bentley, D. D., S. P. A., was eminent as a person of very various attainments in philosophy
and literature, of large acquaintance with books beyond
the range of ordinary reading, extending his researches
to foreign libraries, particularly to oriental sources. He
was deeply interested in geographical studies, and always
zealously engaged in exploring local antiquities; his
multifarious attainments in that line, are illustrated in his
"Description and History of Salem," occasional published
discourses, and especially in the columns of the local
press to which he was a constant contributor. His rare
attainments, great benevolence of life, ardent patriotism,
originality and independence of character, mental activity,
and social spirit, made him altogether a most marked and
interesting personage, gave an impulse to the thoughts of
men, and left a stamp upon the general intelligence of
the community not soon to be effaced or forgotten.

John Dexter Treadwell, M. D., A. A. S., was a man of
strong individuality and impressiveness of character, of
extensive learning outside of, as well as in, his profession,
particularly in the lexicography and interpretation of the
Greek and Hebrew Scriptures. His frank and forcible
expressions as he moved about among the people in his
extensive practice, were suggestive and stimulating to
the mental activities of the community.

Nathaniel Bowditch, LL. D., S. P. A., was President
of the American Academy of Arts and Sciences, and a
Fellow of the Royal Society of London. Similar bodies,
in the great centres of science in foreign countries,
honored themselves by inscribing his great name on their
rolls. He was a writer of recognized authority in
astronomy and kindred departments. His translation of
the "Mecanique Celeste," with the commentary that accom-
panies and gives completeness to it, places his name
where none other stands, by the side of LaPlace. His
"Practical Navigator," cannot be displaced as a standard
work, and will forever guide the sailor over the trackless
deep. As a mathematician he holds the front rank, and
will through all coming time. Dr. Bowditch was not, as
one would suppose from the amount of hard mental work
he performed, a recluse, wholly absorbed by calculation
and the solution of profound problems requiring the
utmost concentration of mind; he was a social, cheerful,
lively man, mixing with the people, more active in practical every day affairs than most persons, with faculties
ever free and fresh, in all neighborly, friendly, and
domestic relations and circles. The influence of such a
character, upon the prevalent ideas of the community in
which he lived cannot be overrated.

To show how fully I am sustained in the reasoning

which these instances are cited to support, the following
passage from Dr. Bowditch's will is presented:

"Item. It is well known, that the valuable scientific
library of the celebrated Dr. Richard Kirwan was, during
the revolutionary war, captured in the British channel,
on its way to Ireland, by a Beverly privateer; and that,
by the liberal and enlightened views of the owners of the
vessel, the library thus captured was sold at a very low
rate; and in this manner was laid the foundation, upon
which has since been successively established, the Philosophical Library, so-called, and the present Salem Athenæum. Thus, in early life, I found near me a better
collection of philosophical and scientific works than could
be found in any other part of the United States nearer
than Philadelphia. And by the kindness of its proprietors I was permitted freely to take books from that
library, and to consult and study them at pleasure. This
inestimable advantage has made me deeply a debtor to
the Salem Athenæum: and I do therefore give to that
Institution the sum of one thousand dollars, the income
thereof to be forever applied to the promotion of its
objects, and the extension of its usefulness."

When we consider that he gave legacies, of the same
amount each, to the Salem Marine Society and the East
India Marine Society, both which institutions had be-
friended him or his relations, and which, in their respective spheres, have done so much to raise the character and
improve the condition of our maritime population, and
take into the account the means and circumstances of the
donor, they cannot but be regarded as noble benefactions,
and demonstrative of the depth of his gratitude.

If Richard Kirwan could have foreseen the testimony
that has just been read, he would have felt his loss more
than remunerated, and, in the magnanimous spirit with
which he refused pecuniary compensation, given thanks

that his books did not reach their destination, but were diverted to this place. If the institutions, whose influence I am sketching, had done no more than open the path through which the mind of Bowditch advanced to its achievements, they would have amply repaid the public-spirited efforts of their founders. But they raised up and stimulated the intellects of many others, as I proceed to show by continuing the list of those who, at the same time, adorned and illuminated this community.

John Pickering, LL. D., S. P. A., was President of the American Academy of Arts and Sciences. As a Greek scholar, and lexicographer he had no superior, and his attainments were great in universal Philology, embracing the languages of continental Europe, and extending to Oriental nations. He had made wide researches also in the aboriginal tongues of America. Foreign scholars recognized his name, and welcomed his labors. He was an honorary member of the Academy of Science and Literature of Palermo, and a corresponding member of the Archæological Society of Athens. He was conversant with general literature, a master of the culture derived from all the fields of classic lore, and, at the same time, a learned and active lawyer. Residence in earlier life in diplomatic circles, at European courts, had added to the natural dignity of his presence, and given a polished refinement to the courtesy and gentleness of his manners. An unobtrusive modesty and simplicity of demeanor, an easy recognition of all pleasant and playful phases of conversation, an affectionate geniality, and a pervading kindness of expression towards all descriptions of persons, made him as fine a specimen of what constitutes the real gentleman as can anywhere be found.

4

Daniel Appleton White, LL. D., A. A. S., was a man
of strong intellectual faculties, highly educated, and of
extensive attainments beyond the range of his profession.
No one among us has been a more earnest or efficient
patron of literary and scientific institutions, and traces
are here to be found, as monuments exist in a sister city
of our county, of his zeal and munificence in the cause
of popular education, and the diffusion of the means of
knowledge. Scholars, philosophers, and distinguished
persons of all sorts, visiting our city, were welcomed to
his generous hospitality, while many an humble, but
aspiring, student felt the cheering and sustaining influence of his liberal sympathy and substantial aid.

Joseph Story, LL. D., A. A. S., S. P. A., trained the
classes in the Law School of our University in all the
learning of his profession, and from the Supreme Bench
of the Union announced, with acknowledged authority,
the interpretation of the Constitution, and the force and
limitation of the Statutes of Nation and State. His
published works exhaust the topics of judicial lore, and
are standard text books in courts at home and abroad.
Besides all this he was a public orator, and shone in
general literary accomplishments. His eloquence and
energy were always at hand to advance the intellectual
condition of the people.

Either of these ten men, all living here together,
would have been recognized as an intellectual leader and
head, in any of our great cities. Combined they were a
constellation rarely equalled, anywhere, in any age.
They were none of them mere bookish men, standing
aloof from the community, but severally among the
people, and of the people ; to be seen daily, as much as
any class of persons, in the streets, social circles, and

places of public resort. They took as active and efficient a part in local affairs as others. They were always in lively contact with their fellow citizens, without reserve, hauteur, or pretension. It is obvious that their influence upon the condition and current of popular thought could not but have been most potent and far reaching.

There were many others, younger men, of marked eminence, adding to the mental stimulus of the place. Leverett Saltonstall, LL. D., A. A. S., did not forget, while in extensive professional practice, to keep a deep interest in the general culture and higher welfare of the community. Education, fine faculties, fluent speech, a generous and magnanimous nature made him a persuasive and impressive speaker at the bar, and in popular assemblies. Literary tastes, the warmth of his heart, sympathy with all amiable human affections, a manly ease and freedom of address gave him a just influence in private circles, and all associated forms of action. He was an enthusiast in whatever relates to colonial or local history, and the memory of the Fathers. One of the founders of the Essex Historical Society, and always an active member, he was selected to deliver the Address, on the 197th anniversary of the landing of Endicott. The occasion was observed, Sept. 6th, 1825, with much public interest, in the meeting-house of the First Church. A large audience appreciated the ability and eloquence of the discourse, which gave an early and efficient impulse to the commemorative spirit now happily pervading the land.

Benjamin Merrill, LL. D., was a learned lawyer and scholar, the influence of whose pleasant humor, polished and pregnant wit, and acuteness and force of thought enlivened conversation and gave effect to the productions of his pen in racy articles, long continuing to add attractiveness to the local press, particularly to the Salem Gazette.

David Cummings, a man of strong powers, and prominent at the bar, is well remembered for his ardent natural eloquence at public meetings and in addresses to juries. His pure and noble spirit, and transparent character, secured the respect and confidence of all, while his genial ingenuousness, freshness of thought and expression, acuteness of perception, keen but playful and benignant satire, and an enthusiasm all his own, delighted every circle in which he moved.

Joseph E. Sprague, was early drawn from legal practice into political life, in which few ever bore a more active or efficient part. His facile, rapid, and felicitous pen was always ready to meet the demands of the hour, not merely for party purposes, but to give expression to worthy sentiments on the topics and occurrences that arrested notice from time to time. Like his classmate Merrill, he fully discharged his obligations to the public by using the columns of the Register to promote the intelligence, and guide the thoughts of the people. Saltonstall and Merrill, on one side, and Cummings and Sprague, on the other, were leading actors in political operations, at a time when party passions were exasperated beyond the experience of our day, but so liberal and enlightened were their spirits that the bonds of personal friendship were never severed between them, and they acted cordially together in giving their sympathy and influence to the general welfare and progress of society.

John Glen King, a learned lawyer, had rare classical attainments, and was widely known as one of the choicest scholars of his period. He studied the writings of the early fathers of the Christian Church to an extent which but few clergymen have equalled.

Reuben Dimond Mussey, M. D., LL. D., A. A. S., was a leading practitioner here, and established a national reputation that ultimately drew him to the West, where he was welcomed as one of the heads of his profession. While in Salem, in 1812 and 1813, he gave courses of lectures on chemistry, imparting such an interest, in this community, to that subject that the thoughts of enterprising business men were particularly turned to it; and as is generally supposed, the Laboratory, incorporated in 1819, which has been in successful operation ever since, manufacturing, on a large scale, aquafortis, muriatic acid, oil of vitriol, blue vitriol and alum, was the result. For many years he had in charge the medical department of Dartmouth College, lecturing on the Theory and Practice of Medicine, Materia Medica, Surgery, and Medical Jurisprudence.

Daniel Oliver M. D., LL. D., A. A. S., was associated with Dr. Mussey in practice, and coöperated in conducting the lectures on chemistry. In 1820, he was elected Professor in the Medical School of Dartmouth College, and also filled the chair of Intellectual and Moral Philosophy there, continuing in the discharge of his duties with high reputation until 1837. Subsequently he was called to a professorship in the college of Ohio. After a brief, but distinguished service in that new and wider field, he was compelled to relinquish his labors by a disease which proved fatal in 1842. He was a learned, able, and accomplished scholar, outside of his profession, of rare attainments in classical, French and German literature. His tastes, manners, and character were eminently refined, delicate and retiring; but there was, notwithstanding, a universal recognition of his merits. His work entitled "First Lines of Physiology," is a standard authority. The leading collegiate institutions of his own country conferred upon him their diplomas, and he was an honorary member of the Academy of Science and Literature at Palermo.

Henry Alexander Scammell Dearborn, A. A. S., after completing his professional preparation in the office of Judge Story, entered upon the practice of law here, and was early brought into particular notice by addresses on public occasions, and articles in leading journals and magazines. His attention was given to Agriculture as a science and art, especially to Horticulture. No one did more to inspire a taste and interest in such subjects, and in recognition of this fact, the municipal authorities, in laying out a street bordered by proprietors engaged in rearing nurseries of trees and flowers, called it by his name. General Dearborn was the first President of the Massachusetts Horticultural Society. The traces of his hand are to be seen at Mount Auburn, and the Forest Hills Cemetery in Roxbury, the place of his residence during much of the latter portion of his life. He was long in the public service in local, state, and national offices. He was the author of valuable works relating to commerce and internal improvements, as well as Agriculture; and in the department of biography, naval and military. He wrote, not so much from ambition in authorship, as from the love of literary occupation, and for the gratification of his sense of the beautiful in art, leaving behind him elaborate, exquisitely finished and embellished manuscript volumes, designed as memorials for his friends and family, on Architecture and Flowers;

31

and also a Life of Christ, in which all the passages of
scripture relating to it, are collected and harmonized into
a continuous narrative.

Joseph Emerson Worcester, LL. D., A. A. S., passed
some years here as a teacher, engaged, at the same time
in preparing his Geographical Dictionary or Universal
Gazetteer. Publications of this class secured him the
honor of election as a corresponding member of the
Royal Geographical Society of London. In the Athenæum and private libraries, and the society of our cultivated men and accurate scholars, he was preparing his
mind for the great work of his life — that monument of
patience, perseverence, judgment, taste and learning —
The Dictionary of the English Language.

Thomas Cole, A. A. S., was a thoroughly trained
scholar and teacher, conversant with the various departments of science and philosophy, particularly astronomy
and meteorology, and occupying the first rank of micro-
scopists, pursuing researches to the minutest recesses of
the fields of natural science.

William Gibbs, shrinking from observation with the
most sensitive modesty and humility, could not escape being recognized as an antiquarian explorer, as
exact, thorough and successful as any we have ever had
among us.

Malthus Augustus Ward, M. D., also a person of unobtrusive deportment, in addition to the learning of his
profession, pursued the science of natural history with a
quiet enthusiasm that conducted him to wide attainments
in that department, especially in botany. He removed to
Athens, in Georgia, and during the residue of his life
was connected with the University there, as Professor in
his favorite branch. In that service he exerted an ex-

tensive influence in behalf of science and learning, conferring lasting benefit upon the young men then passing through the academic course. Among his pupils was Alexander H. Stephens, who has expressed to me in the strongest terms the value he and all others attached to Dr. Ward's instructions, gratefully ascribing to him the credit of directing the studies, guiding the tastes, and stimulating the minds of those frequenting his lecture-rooms and participating in explorations and observations of the surrounding region, over which he was wont to lead them, disclosing the beauties and wonders of nature.

Near the close of the period, to which I am referring, in 1820 and 1821, the corps of our enlightened citizens and highly educated men was reinforced by the settlement here of two distinguished clergymen, John Brazer, D. D., A. A. S., Professor of Latin in Harvard University, a ripe classical scholar, of extensive attainments in general, especially in critical, learning, and a writer of unsurpassed clearness, accuracy, and purity of style; and James Flint, D. D., whose mind was also stored with the treasures of classical, as well as sacred literature. Familiar with the best productions in prose and verse of English authors, bearing in his memory all their finest passages, a rich imagination, and free and fervid expression, gave to his private conversation and public discourses, and to occasional poetic pieces that will never be forgotten, the power of eloquence and the stamp of genius.

All these were either early trained in academic discipline, or mainly devoted to studious pursuits. But there were others, self-educated, and engaged in ordinary occupations of active life, foreign from literature or science, who, like the subject of this memoir, found time, notwithstanding, to gratify a love of knowledge by prosecuting, as a recreation and for their private enjoyment, researches in intellectual and philosophical spheres, and whose habits and attainments were well known, and operated as an incentive to others.

Jonathan Webb, an apothecary, attentive to his busi-. ness and an active and efficient citizen, was an electrician without a superior, retreating, in his leisure hours, to apartments provided for the purpose within his own premises, and filled with apparatus upon which he practiced and experimented, developing the wondrous properties of the element of nature, in whose study he was an enthusiast.

Thomas Spencer, an English emigrant, in the humblest condition, a tallow chandler by trade, and for some time without any means but what were supplied by industrious toil, as a day laborer, after a while became known as a philosophic lover of nature, and a refined and beautiful writer. His lectures, on the forest trees of this neighborhood and on the phenomena of light and the laws of vision, were performances of exquisite finish. Although his condition was originally lowly and obscure, having been born with a pure and gifted genius, and, through all disadvantages, cultivated his mind from childhood, he here soon found friends, and a public that appreciated him. He is still living, his venerable age illuminated by mental and moral accomplishments, an opulent and extensive landholder in one of the richest agricultural counties of England. His history is, indeed, invested with a truly romantic interest. Messages of love, received from time to time, show that he remembers, with affectionate and grateful feelings, the friend-' ship and sympathy he here enjoyed.

There was a young man, employed as a clerk in the

5

counting-rooms of one of our great merchants, afterwards carrying on, for a while, a retail store, whose exuberant spirits made him the life of all companies, in scenes of innocent social gayety, but who early caught the inspiration of the place, and seized every available moment to enrich his mind by the study of the best English works. Upon reaching an adult age he, at once, made himself felt as a devoted supporter of all movements in favor of the diffusion of knowledge ; and to his inspiring activity and contagious enthusiasm, the Essex Historical Society largely owes its origin. After an absence of forty years, during which he was deeply engaged in business, connected with the transaction of extensive commercial affairs, in New York, Europe, and California, he returned with unabated zeal to give, in the last year of his life, an impulse to the Essex Institute it will feel forever. Although always immersed in occupations aside from literature that would have wholly absorbed, if not exhausted, other men, George Atkinson Ward continued the preparation, he here began, to take his place permanently among men of letters. From time to time the productions of his pen gave vivacity to the columns of periodicals ; and he lived to complete the fourth edition of his "Journal and Letters of Samuel Curwen." The writings of Judge Curwen were the products and the evidence of the taste and culture that prevailed here during the last century, and the volume in which Mr. Ward presented them to the public, with the value added by his editorial labors, is secure, I am confident, of holding its place, in all coming time, as a standard work, containing much that illustrates the opening of the revolutionary struggle, and giving the best view that ever has been presented, or can ever be obtained, of the interior social condition of the mother country at that period.

Behind the counter of a retail store, on Essex street, at the period now under review, was to be found a person pursuing the daily routine of a most unpretentious life, apparently thinking of nothing else than the accommodation of customers, in the exhibition of his stock, and measuring out, by the yard, linen, cotton, ribbons and tape. He was, apparently, beyond middle life, of a mild and courteous demeanor, quiet, and of few words. There was, it is true, in his mein and manners, a combined gentleness and dignity, that marked him as differing from the common run of men, but nothing to indicate the tenor of his peculiar mental occupations. The leisure hours of that man were employed in patient, minute, comprehensive and far reaching researches in books, quarterly journals, magazines, and political documents, guided by a cultivated taste, keen discrimination, familiarity with the best models of style and thought, and intimate acquaintance with the biographical details of all the prominent public characters of England, and their personal, family, and party relations to each other, that enabled him to grapple with a subject, that was engrossing and defying the ingenuity of them all, and thereby . to place himself as a peer among the literati of his day. The most critical and distinguished minds, on both sides of the Atlantic, at that time and for a great length of years, were engaged in elaborate and indefatigable efforts to solve a problem, which more and longer, perhaps, than any similar inquisition, has arrested the curiosity and scrutiny of mankind.

A series of letters, from January, 1769, to January, 1772, appeared in a London paper, the "Public Advertiser," over the signature of "Junius," discussing the conduct of the ministers of government, measures of ad-

ministration, and the characters of living statesmen, in a
style of elegance, severity, force and effectiveness, never
surpassed, if ever equalled. They were felt and acknowledged then, as they are now, to be masterpieces, in
grace of diction and power of thought. In the most
wonderful manner their authorship was kept concealed
against a pressure that exhausted every form of vigilance
and espionage that could be brought to bear. As, week
after week, they shook the mind of England and the age
to its centre, and flashed before all eyes, as from a gal-
vanic battery, living pictures of the great men of that
period, of course they became the subject of universal
and most exciting interest, growing deeper and stronger
from day to day. Who is the author of these letters?
was the question on all lips. To give an idea of the
kind of sensation created by them, I present a few speci-
mens of the manner in which their "great unknown"
author is spoken of. The writer of the article on the
subject in the "Encyclopædia Americana," thus charac-
terizes him. "His style is severe, concise, epigrammatic
and polished; his reasoning powerful; his invective un-
sparing and terrible." Again: "He was evidently acquainted, not only with the court, but with the city;
with the history, private intrigues, and secret characters
of the great; with the management of the public offices;
with the proceedings of Parliament (not then, as since,
public); and also with the official underlings, through
whom he sometimes condescends to lash their superiors.
With this extensive information, he united a boldness,
vehemence, and rancor, which, while he spared no one,
stopped at nothing, and rendered him an object of terror
to those whom he attacked. To use his own language,
'he gathers like a tempest, and all the fury of the ele-

ments bursts upon them at once.'" At first the general
suspicion was fixed upon Burke, who alone was thought
capable of such wonderful compositions, but he publicly
denied being their author, and in a speech in the House
of Commons, expressed his opinion of him, "in rancor
and venom, the North Briton is as much inferior to him,
as in strength, wit, and judgment. King, Lords, and
Commons are but the sport of his fury."

Besides Burke, conjecture fell at different times, upon
a great variety of persons, among them the Grenvilles,
Wilkes, Dunning, Charles Lloyd, John Horne Tooke,
Charles Lee, Sir Philip Francis, Hugh Macauley. Boyd,
Gibbon, Grattan, Sir William Jones, Horace Walpole,
Lords Sackville, Camden, Chatham and Chesterfield.

Among the great minds engaged in discussing this
question, and seeking to solve the problem, were Burke,
Lord Eldon, the celebrated Dr. Samuel Parr, Sir William
Draper, Butler the learned English lawyer, and a host of
others. Any number of books were published in England and in America on the subject, and all the literary
and political journals lent their columns to elaborate articles pressing theories, based upon prying research and
industrious investigations. But all attempts to penetrate
the veil, and disperse the shadow the writer had thrown
over his name, failed; but still the search continued with
unabated earnestness.

It is indeed marvellous that a Salem retail shop-keeper,
without any known aid, but from local libraries and the
society of persons here eminently conversant with the
materials that could shed light upon such a subject, was
enabled to enter into this crowd of great contestants for
the discovery of the world-engrossing secret, and bear off
the palm of victory in such a race. But this, in the

judgment of many most competent to give an opinion, Isaac Newhall did. The writer of the article in the Encyclopædia just quoted, sums up a review of the whole ground by citing the "ingenious" volume, as he pronounces it, published by Mr. Newhall, entitled "Letters on Junius," in which the opinion is maintained that the famous documents were from the pen of Lord Temple, brother of George Grenville ; and upon critically examining the evidence presented by Mr. Newhall, declares his hypothesis "probable," saying in conclusion—"if it is not the true one, it is certainly embarrassed with fewer difficulties, than any which have come to our knowledge."

The influence of the examples I have enumerated, heightening the preëxisting tendency of the general intellect and of the then commercial character of the place, which diffused through the whole body of the people knowledge derived from conversance with all nations in all parts of the globe, reached the inmost recesses of society, and was felt in every condition of life. The inspiration was caught by the young, and a bias towards intellectual occupations, and a taste for the pleasures of literature and science, early imparted to many minds. In the opening decades of this century, the eye of a prophet would have detected, in primary and preparatory schools, and among the boys at play in our streets, names now enrolled in the very foremost rank, in the various fields of letters and science. In history—William Hickling Prescott ; the higher mathematics—Benjamin Peirce ; elegant literature in its most attractive departments—Nathaniel Hawthorne ; botany and its kindred branches—John Lewis Russell ; magnetism, electricity and chemistry—Charles Grafton Page ; and poetry in one of its purest forms—Jones Very.

The sketch now given, has been confined to Salem, The theme is equally fruitful, if the field of view is extended over the whole surface of this part of the commonwealth. I leave to others more competent to do it justice, the grateful task of enumerating the strong minds and characters, adorning the early annals of Ipswich in its original dimensions when the great court town, Andover, Haverhill, the other towns on the Merrimack, especially Newburyport in every stage of its history, Lynn, Marblehead, and all over the county. It can thus be shown that the elements of intellectual culture were sown broadcast throughout the region, and that such characters as have now been enumerated, and as we are preparing particularly to consider, are the spontaneous product of our soil.

The "Essex County Natural History Society" was incorporated in 1836. A young man, a native of our city, engaged in business here as a bookseller, Benjamin Hale Ives, inspired with enthusiasm as a naturalist, awakened especial attention to the subject by articles in the newspapers from his pen, continued from time to time until the movement was effectually started. His early death, in 1837, was a great loss to science, and to the community in all its interests. The first President of the Society was Andrew Nichols, M. D., of Danvers, now Peabody. He was born in 1785 and died in 1853. Learned in his profession, and honored for his worth in all respects, he had tastes and faculties that found their gratification in philosophic pursuits—a dear lover of nature—of an imaginative and poetic temperament,—flowers and trees and the fields and forests they adorn, were to him, as he wandered among them, things not only of beauty, but of life. No one ever explored them with more delight or studied them more thoroughly. In 1816, Dr. Nichols gave a course of Botanical Lectures in Salem, and always delighted to communicate information, and awaken interest in that department of knowledge. Zoölogy was also one of his favorite subjects of observation and research. He was naturally the chosen leader of those engaged in these fascinating departments of science.

The "Essex County Historical Society" and the "Essex County Natural History Society" were consolidated, under the name of the "Essex Institute," in 1848. Judge Daniel A. White was the first President.

The Essex Institute is the mature growth of the seed planted here more than a century ago, on ground ready to receive it, which came into full flower, in the cluster of great minds adorning this community half a century since, and whose ripened fruit will perennially and forever, we trust, be gathered by all who reach forth their hands to pluck it. Under the care and guidance of devoted scholars and students, whose labors and lives have been given to it, the Institute has become what it is. Their services are appreciated and honored here and elsewhere. While they, and he, so long their Secretary and now their President, around whom they are encircled, who toils for it by day and watches over it by night, whose learning, science, resources and affections are all merged in it, are here to listen, I must not name them. The eulogist and historian, at a future—may it be a long distant—day will have their memories in charge, and then express the gratitude we now can only feel.

By the published volumes of its "Historical Collections" and "Proceedings," and the "American Naturalist"; its field meetings, and meetings for discussions, written and oral, of matters of science, history and literature;

its horticultural and other exhibitions ; its already extensive library of books, pamphlets and manuscripts, and its
invaluable museum, the Institute has made an achieve-
ment, beginning to be universally recognized. In no
locality, in the country, has so much been accomplished
in exhuming and working the treasures of municipal,
civil, and personal history, and in bringing to light antiquities and natural productions, as in this county. For
all this we are mainly indebted to the Essex Institute.
No writer can trace the origin and history of any of
our towns, or portray a passage of our annals, without
depending upon resources it has provided, while its explorations are covering every department of natural objects
and phenomena.

I have endeavored to explain how the institution and
influence of an association, so efficient in its action,
and already attracting so wide a notice, can be accounted
for, as having been established and wrought to such vigor
in this comparatively small and suburban city. The personal memoir, I am now prepared to present, will exhibit,
in a particular instance, a striking result of the same
operative causes.

Lieutenant Francis Peabody emigrated to this country,
at about twenty-one years of age, from St. Albans, Hert-
fordshire, England, in 1635. He is stated to have first
settled in Ipswich, which then included, indefinitely, the
territory outside of the present limits of that town to and
beyond the Merrimack river. His name is found; as of
the grand jury, and on trial juries, from Hampton. As
that place was finally decided to be within the limits of
New Hampshire, and as he also desired to be "nearer
Boston," he sold his estate in Hampton in 1650, and
bought land in what is now Topsfield, on its southern

6

line, near Governor Endicott's Ipswich River farm, where he spent the remainder of his days. By his wife Mary, daughter of Reginald Foster, he had fourteen children, and died in February, 1698, at the age of eighty-four.

His fourth son, Isaac, was born in 1648. The homestead was assigned to him. He died in 1726.

His eldest son, Francis, was born, December 1st, 1694, bore the military title of Cornet, and lived in Middleton, where he died April 23d, 1769.

His eldest son Francis, born September 21st, 1715, was Deacon of the church in Middleton, and died there, December 7th, 1797.

His sixth son, Joseph, was born December 12th, 1757, and died January 5th, 1844. He was one of the most eminent merchants of his day, carrying on a commerce that encircled the globe, and making this port the point of arrival and departure of his richly laden fleet. His eldest son, Joseph Augustus, born in 1796, was graduated at Harvard College in 1816, but commerce was the profession of his choice. His position made him familiar with the business, and he had the qualities enabling him to take the place of his father. The prospects of this town, as connected with foreign trade and its maritime welfare, were considered by the people as identified with him. His pure and amiable character was recognized and appreciated by all; and deep was the sense of a great public misfortune, when he was taken away, in 1828. The day of his funeral, as I well remember, was one of general mourning. The second son of Joseph Peabody, Charles, born December 8th, 1797, was drowned August 10th, 1805. The third named Francis, born July 14th, 1799, died in infancy. The fourth, also named Francis, was born December 7th, 1801, and is the subject of the present memoir; he was of the fifth descent from the founder of the family in America, and bore his name. His mother was Elizabeth, daughter of the Rev. Elias Smith of Middleton.

At ten years of age he was placed in Dummer Academy, at Byfield, under the care of the Rev. Abiel Abbott, D. D., a graduate of Harvard College in the class of 1787, originally pastor of a church in Coventry, Connecticut, subsequently at Peterboro', N. H., and whose last years were passed at West Cambridge, where he died in 1859, at the age of ninety-four—one of the best of scholars and of men, loved and revered by his pupils, and honored by all in the varied scenes of his active service. At about twelve years of age, young Peabody was removed to Brighton, where he passed about four years in a select private school, kept by Jacob Newman Knapp, of the Harvard class of 1802 ; a man of eminent reputation as a scholar and instructor, and especially remembered, as such, by our elderly people. He opened a school here more than sixty-five years ago, Jan. 1, 1803, which continued until 1811. Through his long protracted life, there has been no failure of vigor or activity, his physical and mental powers remaining wholly unimpaired.*

Through his school days, and indeed from early childhood, Francis Peabody gave indications of the tendency of mind that so strikingly marked his maturer years. He was ever exercising his constructive faculties, making miniature machines, trying experiments upon the objects and forces of nature within his reach, and occupy-

---

* Mr. Knapp died July 27th, 1868, at Walpole, N. H., aged ninety-four years and eight months.

ing all the hours, when free from regular and appointed tasks, in contrivances, manipulations, and drawings.

His regular academic education terminated with his residence at Brighton, and he returned to his home in Salem. The prevalent direction of his thoughts, as just indicated, disinclined him to the general exercises of collegiate establishments. Their purpose is to take the mind before it has received a controlling bias to any particular branch of knowledge, and lead it through the whole circle; make it try all, survey the entire field, and then select for its life-pursuit what it thus finds in most affinity with its own special tastes and faculties. He had found, by tendencies that could not be overruled, and convictions that could not be called into question, even in his earliest boyhood, in what path his mind was designed to travel, and he entered upon it, at once. More than this, his extraordinary activity and mobility of temperament, made the thought of the slow routine and measured pace of collegiate life quite repulsive; and it was wisely concluded not to enforce upon him the completion of his education, by residence in the ordinary way, and for the usual time, at the university. He was allowed, and enabled, to gratify his predilection for scientific and mechanical operations at home; and entered at once, in his own way, upon chemical processes, and the ingenious use of machinery and methods of operation; which, however, before long, were interrupted by a violent sickness in the form of typhus fever, that, for some time, threatened his life, and from which he slowly recovered.

For the purpose of fully reëstablishing his health, a sea voyage was deemed expedient, and he made his first trip across the Atlantic. Early in the summer of 1820, when eighteen years of age, he took passage in one of his father's ships, the Augustus, to Russia. She was commanded by John Endicott Giddings of Beverly; Jonathan Flint was first mate, Oliver Thayer, second mate, and Samuel Endicott, Jr., supercargo. The crew, as was then almost always the case, was composed of young men belonging to the place and neighborhood. Of course all care was taken to provide everything that would be agreeable or beneficial to a young person not yet entirely relieved of the character of an invalid. Among other things a goat was placed on board for his special comfort and nourishment. The vessel, as usual, made the northern passage, touching at a solitary rocky islet, about half-way between the Orkney and Shetland groups. The nearest land is Samburg Ness, the southern extremity of the Shetlands, from which point its lofty crags are visible. From the island itself nothing is in sight, all around, but the dreary desert ocean. For what reason I know not, nor can imagine, the place is called Fair Island, and, as such, is put done on the maps. It is four miles in length, and two and a half in breadth; and has but one harbor. Its inhabitants are excluded from all cognizance of the rest of the world, except when, as in this case, a passing vessel comes to, in their port. This small desolate spot, alone and a-far-off, in so high a latitude, in the midst of a comparatively unfrequented sea, whose wild storms almost throw their spray over the whole island from shore to shore, has, of course, but a small population, necessarily destitute of many of the comforts of life. Whenever the rare opportunity occurs, they gather upon the deck of the transient visitor, and seek to get what they can; and as they have nothing to give in exchange, have naturally become inveterate beggars. The young passenger, commiserating their destitute condition, and moved by their forlorn entreaties, parted with whatever he could possibly spare of his stores and wardrobe; and to one old man who told a pitiful tale of the infirmities of his sick, famishing, and aged wife, he relinquished his goat. This circumstance, for which I am indebted to our esteemed fellow citizen, Captain Oliver Thayer, is mentioned because it illustrates a trait of character, that may be fittingly noticed in this connection, which Francis Peabody exhibited through life. A more kind and obliging disposition never existed, as all, who have had occasion to be its objects, gratefully remember.

When the vessel was lying at Cronstadt, Mr. Peabody, accompanied by a son of the American Minister at St. Petersburg, made an extensive tour into the interior of Russia, visiting Moscow and other chief points of interest.

Coming home, on her return trip, in the same vessel, he devoted himself, with renewed health and zeal, to his laboratory. The next winter he attended a course of scientific lectures, at Boston, passing regularly over the Turnpike, in all weathers. The next he spent, for the same purpose, in Philadelphia, frequenting its scientific rooms, especially that of Dr. Hare, with whom he formed an acquaintance that soon assumed, and ever after retained, the character of an intimate and mutual personal attachment.

On the 7th of July, 1823, he was married to Martha Endicott, of the seventh descent from the original Governor of the Plantation. Her father, Samuel Endicott, was born, as all his intermediate ancestors had been, on the Orchard Farm.

At every period of his life, while mainly occupied in
his favorite studies and pursuits, he was led by the extraordinary activity of his nature, to participate with his
whole soul, in whatever was going on around him, in
social movements and local interests, that commended
themselves to his favorable judgment. About this time
his attention was given, with great enthusiasm, to military matters, inheriting the true spirit of a New Eng-
lander, transmitted through his ancestors, who had borne
titles of honor in rural trainbands. He commanded a
battalion of Artillery, and was soon promoted to a
Lieutenant-Colonelcy, in that arm. In 1825, he was
transferred to the Infantry, as Colonel of the 1st Reg.,
1st Brig., 2d Div., Massachusetts militia. It was probably much owing to his energy and zeal in the service,
that the famous muster, and sham fight, well remembered
by our older citizens, took place near Tapley's Brook, in
what was then Danvers, on the 6th of October, 1826, in
which five regiments of Infantry, one regiment and a
battalion of artillery, and a battalion of cavalry took
part. Ten light companies were included in the force
brought into array on the occasion. The broad plains on
both sides of the old road to Lynn, at that point, afforded
favorable ground for evolutions, manœuvrings, display,
skirmishes, and battle. It was the last great affair of the
kind, under the old militia system, when the whole male
population, with limited exceptions, within the military
age, was enrolled and mustered. There was an entire
regiment from Marblehead and another from Beverly.
Of the scene exhibited that day I can speak, for I bore
part in it, as chaplain of Colonel Peabody's regiment.
He had provided me with sword, belt, sash, and the
chapeau bras then worn by commissioned, especially

field and staff, officers, and sent a horse to my door. In company with Charles Gideon Putnam, Assistant Surgeon of the Regiment, now President of the Massachusetts Medical Society, I sought a position on a neighboring height. As we were non-combatants and our services would not be needed until casualties occurred, we thought it best to be out of the reach of stray ramrods. The whole ground was spread out to our view, and under a bright, but tempered sun, it was worth beholding. An uncounted multitude darkened the distant acclivities and the level area all around outside of the lines. The roar of artillery, the incessant rattling of infantry fire, the clouds of smoke, the dashing onsets of trampling cavalry, and the final desperate charge by bayonet and sabre of the contending forces simultaneously along the whole line, made the mimic battle complete.

Having exhausted the activities of a military life, it had no charm left for Francis Peabody, and he forthwith gave himself back to his predominating tastes, and to the inexhaustible satisfactions they afforded him. Yielding again, and now once for all, to the spirit of the place, he renewed his philosophical and inventive operations, and engaged in branches of business, manufacturing and commercial, to which they led him; remaining always on hand, however, to bear his part in movements for the general welfare.

I shall sketch his progress somewhat in the order of time, but not undertaking to enter into details; that would require many extended scientific treatises, and explanations and illustrations altogether beyond allowed limits on this occasion.

In 1826 he was mainly occupied in experiments, studies, and calculations connected with the establish-

ment of a business he long carried on, upon a large
scale, which has passed into the hands and is now conducted by the "Forest River Lead Company."

Colonel Peabody was among the first to introduce the
system of miscellaneous courses of public lectures on
scientific and literary subjects, which has since been
developed into one of the most efficient agents in advanc-
ing the intelligence and general civilization of the people
of this country. On the 6th of November, 1827, the
Essex Lodge of Freemasons in Salem voted to have a
series of literary and scientific lectures, which commenced
in January, 1828, and continued to May. Among the
lecturers were Thomas Cole, George Choate, Francis
Peabody, Jonathan Webb, Malthus A. Ward, and Benjamin F. Browne.

About the same time the Salem Charitable Mechanic
Association appointed a committee to provide lectures
for the members and their families. On the 24th of
January, 1828, the introductory lecture was delivered by
Dr. George Choate, who was followed by Caleb Foote,
N. J. Lord, John Codman, J. T. Buckingham of Boston,
and others.

During the same season Colonel Peabody gave a free
course of public lectures in Franklin Hall, on the history
and uses of the Steam Engine ; and the next season he
gave a similar course, in coöperation with Jonathan
Webb, on Electricity, in Concert Hall. The display of
apparatus, in the course on Electricity, was extensive and
complete. The exhibition of machinery in connection
with the Steam Engine, provided at the cost of Colonel
Peabody, was finer and larger probably than any ever
presented in this country. People of all conditions were
attracted to the halls, and great interest awakened in

7

such subjects. Young men, especially those in mechanical employments, appreciated the opportunity, and all were instructed. Among them, it may be mentioned, was Increase Sumner Hill, who is now, and long has been, one of the most distinguished mechanical engineers in America, and recognized as such by the government in the commission he has held for many years, as "United States Inspector of Steam Engines and Boilers."

These numerous lectures awakened, in the whole community, a sense of the value of knowledge and of the importance of its diffusion, which, the very next year took form in the establishment of Lyceums—that is, permanent institutions, for the diffusion of knowledge, by miscellaneous lectures—here and elsewhere through the country. A full history of the proceedings, that led to this result, is a subject that deserves, and will undoubtedly receive, a distinct treatment. I can only touch a few points, such as particularly belong to, or are suggested by, my subject.

Near the close of the year 1829, a notice appeared in the newspapers calling a general meeting to be held at Topsfield, for the purpose of establishing a County Lyceum. What the precise object or plan of those concerned in the call was, could not be gathered from its terms. It was understood, however, that it was designed to provide for lectures to be delivered in that, or some other central place, upon which the people of the county were expected to attend. But it was obvious that an institution of the kind could hardly be made to operate efficiently over so wide an area; and much discussion arose touching the proper manner of bringing the process of lecturing to bear upon the people. The consequence was that a large concourse of gentlemen of influence attended the meeting, which was held in the Academy Hall, at Topsfield, on Wednesday, the 30th of December, 1829. I do not remember ever to have witnessed a more interesting and enlightened assembly. Very animated, earnest and protracted debates took place, and it was finally decided by a full, but close vote, that a County Lyceum, if formed at all, ought to consist of delegates chosen in local Lyceums to be previously established in the several towns and villages. A committee was raised to prepare a circular, a duty assigned to me, to be distributed widely throughout the county, setting forth the advantages that would arise from the organization of such institutions, at all points where an adequate population existed; and a day was fixed for delegates, appointed as aforesaid, to meet and form a County Lyceum. Among those acting a prominent part, at the meeting in Topsfield, were Robert Rantoul, Sr. of Beverly, Rev. Gardner B. Perry of Bradford, Rev. Leonard Withington of Newbury, Rev. Henry C. Wright of West Newbury, Dr. Jeremiah Spofford of East Bradford, now Groveland, Isaac R. How of Haverhill, Rev. Charles C. Sewall of Danvers, and Ichabod Tucker, the Rev. James Flint, D. D., David Cummins, Elisha Mack, George Choate, George Wheatland, Francis Peabody, David Roberts, and Robert Rantoul, Jr., of Salem. A Lyceum had previously been established in Beverly. The gentlemen who had attended the meeting from other places, on returning to their respective towns, immediately applied themselves to carry out its resolves, and the result was the formation of such institutions, in every large town, and populous neighborhood in the county.

Such an entire change has come over the spirit of society, since these institutions have been put into operation, owing, I doubt not, very much to their influence, that it is impossible for the present generation to estimate or account for the excitement attending, or the resistance made to their introduction. Great activity and energy were required to bring the public mind to appreciate the movement. In this place the end was accomplished by the earnest enthusiasm of particular persons, among the most zealous of whom was the subject of this memoir. The comparatively early death of Robert Rantoul, Jr., authorizes me specially to refer to him with the gratitude due to his services on this occasion. He gave to the cause the whole force of those faculties which subsequently commanded eminent distinction, among the public men of the commonwealth and country, not only as a politician and legislator, but in the higher fields of philanthrophy and education.

On Monday evening, January 4th, 1830, a meeting was held at the house of Colonel Peabody, at which the following persons, of this place, were present : Daniel A. White, Ichabod Tucker, A. L. Peirson, Malthus A. Ward, Elisha Mack, David Roberts, N. J. Lord, S. P. Webb, R. Rantoul, Jr., Eben Shillaber, G. Wheatland, B. Tucker, Warwick Palfray, John Walsh, Benjamin Crowninshield, Stephen C. Phillips, Jonathan Webb, W. P. Endicott and Caleb Foote. After full and free consultation, it was voted, on motion of Dr. Peirson, "that it is expedient to establish an institution in Salem, for the purpose of mutual instruction and rational entertainment, by means of lectures, debates," &c. On the 11th of January, a public meeting was held in the Town Hall to promote the same object; and on the 18th, at a meeting in Pickering Hall, the Lyceum was formed, and a President, Vice President, Recording Secretary, Corresponding Secretary, and Treasurer, were chosen. At an adjourned meeting, at the same place, on the 20th, a Board of Directors was elected. These meetings were numerously attended, great interest was manifested, and the elections, by ballot, were accompanied by a lively contest between the supporters of different tickets.*

Great difficulty was experienced in procuring a suitable place for the public meetings of the society, and the delivery of the lectures. Attempts were first made to obtain permission to use the Town Hall. Two or three regularly warned, and quite fully attended town meetings, were held on the subject, and much discussion had, but the application failed. The first lecture, by the President, Judge White, a very able performance, the publication of which was immediately called for, was delivered in the Methodist Church, in Sewall street. A gentleman from Andover, Samuel Merrill, Esq., who came all the way to hear it, expressed the universal sentiment of those who listened to, or have read it, in a well turned and indefinitely self-multiplying compliment, when he thanked the Judge at its close, and said in the fulness of his cordial admiration, that he could not tell which had exceeded, his expectations, or the realization.

The society at once became so large that it was necessary to find some other place of meeting, and the subsequent lectures of the course were delivered in the Universalist church. During the next summer a site was

---

* The officers elected, at the meetings of January 18th and 20th, were as follows : — President, Daniel A. White; Vice President, Stephen C. Phillips; Recording Secretary, Stephen P. Webb; Corresponding Secretary, Charles W. Upham; Treasurer, Francis Peabody.

DIRECTORS : — Leverett Saltonstall, George Choate, William Williams, Rufus Babcock, Malthus A. Ward, Abel L. Peirson, Jonathan Webb, Rufus Choate, Caleb Foote, John Moriarty.

purchased and the Lyceum Building erected. Judge White advanced the requisite funds and Colonel Peabody was chairman of the building committee. In many respects the structure was an improvement upon any before, or elsewhere, erected for such purposes, and maintains its reputation and usefulness to this day. The limited dimensions of the site made it too small to accommodate the whole body of members, who had to be divided into two classes; and the lecture, each week, was repeated on the succeeding evening. For several years no compensation was asked by the lecturers, and the proceeds of the sale of tickets soon cleared the property. No undertaking of the kind, or of any kind of associated enterprise, in this place, has been more successful, and the value of the services of the first President, Daniel A White, first Vice President, Stephen C. Phillips, and first Treasurer, Francis Peabody, cannot be overstated.

There had been a few similar institutions elsewhere before. That in Beverly has been mentioned. Bernard Whitman, whose memory is dear to all who knew him, and must be cherished forever by the friends of truth and progress, had, in 1826, established what he called a Rumford Institute, in Waltham, and there were one or two others, in portions of Worcester and Middlesex counties. But it may safely be said that the proceedings at Topsfield and here, originated the institution as a diffusive energy over the country at large. The very next winter there was a legislative public meeting in the hall of the House of Representatives, in the State House, at which the Governor, Levi Lincoln, presided, for the express purpose of promoting the formation of Lyceums throughout the State, in its several cities, towns and villages. They have now been in operation, all over the country, for well nigh forty years ; and it is for the philosophical historian, to consider and estimate their bearings upon the intellectual, social and moral condition of the whole people. It cannot be questioned that they are a potent engine to accelerate the civilization, and raise the level of society.

The first two courses of lectures were as follows. No. 6 of the second course was delivered in the Lyceum Hall, at its opening, and was especially prepared for the occasion.

FIRST COURSE.

1. Feb. 24, 1830, by D. A. White.—The Advantages of Knowledge.
2. March 3, —— " John Brazer.—Authenticity of Ancient Manuscripts.
3. " 10, —— " Francis Peabody.—Steam Engine.
4. " 17, —— " A. L. Peirson.—Physiology.
5. " 24, —— " George Choate.—Geology.
6. " 31, —— " Thomas Spencer.—Optics.
7. April 6, —— " Charles G. Putnam.—Nervous System.
8. " 13, —— " Thomas Cole.—Astronomy.
9. " 20, —— " [a lecture by E. Everett, on a Workingmen's Party, was read by Stephen C. Phillips].
10. " 27, —— " Stephen C. Phillips.—Public Education, with a sketch of the origin of public schools in Salem.
11. May 4, —— " Henry Colman.—Human Mind.
12. " 11, —— " Joshua B. Flint, Boston.—Respiration.
13. " 18, —— " " " " —Circulation of Blood.
14. " 25, —— " " " " —Digestion.

SECOND COURSE.

1. Dec. 1, 1830, by Rufus Babcock.—Power of Mind.
2. " 8, —— " A. H. Everett, Boston.—Review of the continual progress of the improvement of Mankind.
3. " 15, —— " Alonzo Potter, Boston.—Moral Philosophy.
4. " 29, —— " Malthus A. Ward.—Gardening.
5. Jan. 12, 1831, " Leonard Withington, Newbury.—Historical Probability.

6. Jan.   20, 1831, by Stephen C. Phillips.—The influence of the country and the age on the condition of Mankind.

7. "   25-26, —— " Henry K. Oliver.—Pneumatics.

8. Feb. 1-2, —— " A. L. Peirson.—Biography of Dr. Jenner, and History of Vaccination.

9. "   8-9, —— " Henry K. Oliver.—Solar Eclipse of 1831.

10. " 15-16, —— " George Choate.—Climate and its influence on organic life.

11. " 22-23, —— " Charles W. Upham.—Salem Witchcraft.

12. Mch. 1-2, —— "   "   "   "   "

13. "   8-9, —— " Jonathan Webb.—Electricity.

14. " 15-16, —— "   "   "   "

15. " 22-23, —— " A. H. Everett, Boston.—French Revolution.

16. " 29-30, —— "   "   "   "   "   "

17. April 5-6, —— " Thomas Spencer.—Optical Instruments.

18. " 12-13, —— " Malthus A. Ward.—Natural History.

19. " 19-20, —— "   "   "   "

20. " 26-27, —— " Francis Peabody.—Heat.

21. May 3-4, —— " Stephen P. Webb.—Russian History.

22. " 10-11, —— " Edward Everett, Charlestown. — Political Prospects of Europe.

23. " 17-18, —— " Benjamin F. Browne.—Zoölogy.

24. " 24-25, —— " Rufus Choate.—History of Poland.

Before leaving this subject I desire to call attention to the fact, that of the twenty-three gentlemen who took part, as lecturers, in the first two courses, all but five were our own townsmen. This was in accordance with the original design of the institution, which was to develop materials existing among us, encourage home talent, and, here especially, to keep in vigorous action the transmitted love of knowledge. The rapid spread of the system of public lectures, on a permanent footing, very soon led to the formation of a new professional class seeking employment at large. For some years past persons of this description have almost exclusively been called from abroad to lecture in our halls. I would not discourage this practice by other associations, but respectfully suggest whether it would not be well for the Salem Lyceum to return to the original plan. If the Directors should seasonably seek out young men, belonging to our own community, and induce them to select subjects, with the whole intervening period between the courses for research and preparation, I am confident that elements enough could be found in our midst to provide lectures from year to year, that would renew the original interest of the whole people, and, for all reasons, prove widely attractive. Let the experiment be tried. It would, I am quite sure, lead to results in which all would be gratified, carry still higher, from year to year, the standard of general intelligence, and perpetuate the scientific and literary reputation and preëminence of our city.

About the year 1833, Colonel Peabody built the Paper Mills in Middleton. Afterwards he commenced, on a large scale, the business of refining Sperm and Right Whale Oil, and the manufacture of candles. He also erected Linseed Oil Mills at Middleton. In initiating these various branches of business he carried out the results of experiments made in his private laboratory. Much of the machinery, and many of the methods of operation, in all of them, were derived from scientific works in his library, and from the application of his inventive and contriving faculties, under philosophical principles, to the minutest as well as the most complicated details.

Early in 1837, he took a leading part in the preliminary consultations that led to the establishment of the Harmony Grove Cemetery. He presided at the first public meeting, held in Lyceum Hall, February 24th, 1837, to promote the object. Proceedings were interrupted for a time. At a public meeting, September 6th, 1839, he was made chairman of a committee to purchase

8

the grounds. On the 4th of October, 1839, a committee, of which he was also chairman, was entrusted with the superintendency of the work, and under its direction the ground was laid out, with avenues and paths. He prepared the model of the keeper's house; and the rustic arch and gate-way, at the eastern entrance, was planned by him, and constructed under his immediate inspection, combining all the solidity and simplicity that stone can give, with a vestment of living verdure, ever thickening, as the tendrils spread and clasp it, from year to year. He is the first named in the Act of Incorporation, passed February 19, 1840; and his taste, judgment, and active service were appreciated by his associates throughout.

With the subject of architecture, in its character as a science, he had made himself specially and thoroughly acquainted by the study of authorities, and careful observations in his frequent and extensive foreign travels. In what is called Decorative Architecture he had no superior. The construction of his buildings, and the conveniences and adornments of them, were all his own. The arrangements, in detail, of his town house, display his unsurpassed taste, skill, and genius, in this department. His elegant seat at Kernwood, and the configuration and style of the grounds, with all their embellishments, and all their utilities, were from plans prepared by him. Some articles of furniture were selected and purchased abroad, but a large proportion of them, in each of his residences, were from models devised, or drawings executed by his direction, in his workshop, under his own eye, and to a considerable extent, by his own hands. In many particulars of beauty, richness and convenience, they have rarely been equalled. The ornamentation of the interior of the North Church in this city — so much and justly admired — walls, ceiling, orchestra, organ frame, gallery and lights — was wholly designed by him, and executed under his sole direction. His Wind-mill, a skilfully planned and very ingenious machine, upon novel principles, is much used in some of the Western States. The entire structure revolves to meet the direction of the current of air. The fans, of boards or plank, adjust themselves to the force of the wind, and, in fact, the entire machinery works more smoothly, steadily and equably, the stronger it blows. One of them, on the estate at Kernwood, draws from a well, at some distance, and a depth of sixty feet, all the water used in that establishment. Another, a flour mill, constructed on similar principles, but of much larger dimensions, stands on the same premises.

The application of science to practical and useful arts was not only the unwearied labor, but the happy entertainment of his life. For only a few of his innumerable improvements in this department did he procure patent rights, and only in some of them prosecute the results of his contrivances, in actual business operations for the sake of emolument. From time to time many ingenious coöperatives were employed by him, and have derived benefits to themselves, in subsequent periods of their lives, and in other spheres of action, from processes wrought out in his laboratory and workshop, by his and their joint labors, but at his expense. His habit was, when a new subject of research, or the possibility of effecting any particular improvement in the use of mechanical or chemical forces, occurred to him, to learn, in the first instance, all that had been written or accomplished by others in the matter. He would send abroad for the best and latest publications relating to it, and

procure, at any cost, all drawings, descriptions, or instruments that would illustrate it. In this way he collected
a library and apparatus of the choicest and most valuable
sort, and of the greatest variety and extent. After
studying the whole subject, in the use of these means, he
would betake himself to his laboratory, and never weary
in experiments and operations until he had accomplished
the desired result, or become convinced that it was beyond
attainment. As soon, in any case, as the requisite conditions were secured and the designed machine completed,
or the attempt found impracticable, he would turn to
some other project. The consequence is that he has left,
to be used by others, the fruits of his toils. His musical
instruments, for instance, constructed upon the most
ingenious principles, have never been put to use, or
brought before the public ; and the melodeons and organs
constructed by him in the most finished, compact, simple,
economical and beautiful forms, adapted either to pipes
or reeds, in which the use of the fingers of the per-
former, or the hands of a blower, may be dispensed with,
are to be seen only in his own private manufactory.
They were the results of the studies, contrivances and
labors of his last years, and had just been completed.

He had no ambition to acquire celebrity as a man of
science, but only aimed to gratify his own mind in the
pursuit of knowledge, and to turn his experiments and
researches to practical and useful purposes. His active
devotion to philosophical enquiries and operations, did
not, however, escape observation. His zealous labors
were appreciated by all engaged in similar investigations,
and interested in scientific culture and advancement. A
quarter of a century ago he was elected a member of the
American Academy of Arts and Sciences.

In the course of his life, he made, I believe, no less than eight visits to Europe, some of them quite protracted. In most cases his family accompanied him. They were not made to escape from the tediousness of life at home, or to conform with the fashion of people in like circumstances with himself, but for purposes of health, in the gratification of his active nature, and to gather materials for the better development of his zeal for scientific improvement. While abroad he was always on the watch to find and explore whatever illustrated the application of philosophical principles to useful arts, and to keep up ·with the progress of mechanism. He was recognized, as a familiar acquaintance, in the workshops of ingenious artisans in all the great cities, and wherever the processes of skill and ingenuity, in the analysis of the elements of nature and the application of its capacities and forces, were carried to the highest exemplification ; and he would come back to his own laboratory with renewed enthusiasm, wider views, more enlarged knowledge, and more earnest desires to turn to practical account the discoveries of the age.

His attention, on one of these occasions, for instance, while in Paris, was drawn to aluminium, and the properties it possesses. He procured a quantity of the metal upon which to experiment on his return. Some time after reaching home he carried a parcel of it to our respected fellow citizen, Dr. J. E. Fisk, and gave it to him, saying that it was susceptible of a use that would revolutionize the art of dentistry. Dr. Fisk carried out his suggestions, and aluminium is now generally used everywhere, superseding silver, and from it lightness preferable to gold. I mention this, not merely because it shows how Colonel Peabody occupied his thoughts, and exercised his observation while abroad, and the free and liberal use he made of the new ideas there obtained, but also because it presents a singular instance of several minds, placed beyond possible intercommunication, being simultaneously led to the same discovery. When Colonel Peabody made his communication to Dr. Fisk, he supposed that the suggestion was peculiar to himself, and they both took the matter in hand, of the application of aluminium to the particular purpose conjectured, with all the interest and earnestness attending an original experiment. The Doctor found the result perfectly successful, and introduced the great improvement into his practice. But the next "Dental News Letter," the periodical journal of that branch of the Medical Profession, contained an article which showed that Dr. Van Denburgh, of Oswego, New York, at the very time when Dr. Fisk was making out of the lump Colonel Peabody had brought to him for the purpose dental plates of pure aluminium, was doing the same thing without any suspicion that the thought had occurred to another person; and it turned out that, four years before, a patent had been granted in England to a dentist there, for the same object, but that no general publicity, at least out of England, had been given to the improvement. We have here, therefore, a case, in which three minds, entirely separate from each other, travelling over different paths, came together at the same point, in an application of scientific research, to a discovery of great practical importance.

At this point it may be most proper, as the review of Colonel Peabody's operations, in the search of scientific truth, and in effectual applications of it in manufacturing and commercial pursuits, is drawing to a close, to insert the following letters, addressed to me, from persons whose recollections specially enable them to speak upon the subject :

"EAST, BOSTON, MASS., March 16, 1868.

Your note of the 14th inst., in reference to my recollections of the scientific lectures of our late esteemed friend, Francis Peabody, during the years 1828 and 1829, is before me.

In reply, I can only state, that at the time named, I was about twenty-one years of age, and was beginning to be interested in the *Steam Engine*, and in Natural Philosophy generally. A few years previous to these dates, I became acquainted with Joseph Dixon (now of Jersey City, N. J.), and with him generally attended Mr. Peabody's lectures in Salem. At that time, being somewhat acquainted with practical mechanics, I was frequently employed by Mr. Peabody in repairing or constructing some of his apparatus, which embraced all that was then known of the *Steam Engine, Electricity, Pneumatics, Hydraulics, Chemistry*, etc., but Mr. Dixon was his *right hand* man, and had the general management and manipulation of all Mr. Peabody's apparatus during the progress of the lectures, thereby relieving Mr. Peabody from making the experiments himself before the audience, and giving Mr. Dixon the opportunity of manipulating, at which he was an *expert* and entirely at home.

From my long acquaintance and unbroken intimacy with Colonel Peabody, I formed the opinion that he possessed a vast fund of theoretical knowledge upon all the subjects before named, and as a *practical* Chemist, he occupied the front rank. In his later years he frequently ultimated this knowledge in various kinds of manufactures, which seemingly was the love of his life. He was ever of a genial and happy disposition, and nothing gave him greater satisfaction than to be able to answer any questions relating to these interesting subjects.

I am, Sir, most respectfully,

Yours, etc.,

INCREASE S. HILL,

U. S. Inspector of Steam Vessels.

In a letter recently received in this city, from Mr. Dixon, the gentleman referred to by Mr. Hill, he says of Colonel Peabody, that he "had great love for chemical and mechanical knowledge, and a high appreciation of whatever seemed a step forward, in the practical application of science to the arts."

The following is from James Kimball, Esq., President of the Salem Charitable Mechanic Association:

"SALEM, March, 25th, 1868.

Understanding that you have accepted the invitation of the Essex Institute to prepare a Memoir of the late Colonel Francis Peabody, it has been suggested to me, that I give you my recollections of his connection with the introduction of popular lectures as a means of instruction, in the various departments of Scientific Investigation.

In December, 1827, the Mechanic Association of Salem, appointed a Committee to consider the expediency of instituting a course of lectures; at this time I was the acting librarian of the Mechanic Library, and had the opportunity of knowing the views of those most interested in their establishment, and their report, favorable to the proposed object, was based upon the encouragement and coöperation tendered to them by Colonel Peabody, who entered with all the enthusiasm of his nature into the work, and commenced the preparation of a series of lectures on Steam, and its application to the Mechanic Arts.

The first series of lectures delivered by him was in the Franklin Hall. They were practical, as well as experimental, and were illustrated by his valuable and extensive working models. Some of his Steam Engines were of sufficient power to run a common lathe.

I remember well that, in his illustrations of the application of steam as a motive power, he exhibited all the improvements, of any note, that had been made up to that period, with working models of the various inventions from the earliest and simplest application of steam as a motive power, up to the later discoveries and inventions of Watt and others.

It was understood, at that time, that no public institution could exhibit so varied and valuable a collection of working models as Mr. Peabody possessed and used in the illustration of these lectures.

The next season he prepared a Course of Lectures on Chemistry, Electricity, and Pneumatics, in which he was assisted by Dr. Jonathan Webb, a practical chemist and apothecary of that day. These were delivered in Concert Hall, on Central street, and were illustrated by the apparatus of Mr. Peabody. In his lectures on Electricity he used a new machine constructed for himself, which was said to have been the largest in the country; the glass plate wheel of which he had imported from Germany, at great cost. I think it was stated to be $1,500.

Colonel Peabody was admitted a member of the Mechanic Association in 1833, and styled himself a manufacturer.

I feel very confident that the influence of these lectures, on the
young mechanics of that day, was productive of greater good than all
other sources of investigation and study which had ever before been
opened to them, awakening and stimulating the mind by their freshness,
and by the practical application of principles which were new to them,
and but for the interest of the lecturer in the investigation of theories
as well as principles, and his desire to impart to others whatever
interested himself, would have lost a part of their usefulness by being
hid from those who were most likely to be benefited.

I have frequently, since that time, met those who attended these
early lectures, who have referred to them as being their incentives to
further study and investigation; and many of those who have distinguished themselves as master mechanics and inventors, have attributed much of their success to the opportunities afforded, and the
inspiration given them, by the interest taken in their instruction by
one who was desirous of imparting to others whatever his means and
advantages had enabled him to accomplish.

I have thus presented to you my recollections of this period, and
feel very confident that I have not overstated, but have rather come
short of the facts. If they will aid you, in the least, they are at your
service.

Our associate, Henry M. Brooks, clerk of the Forest
River Lead Company, has kindly communicated the
following minutes :

' " Colonel Peabody commenced the White Lead business somewhere
about 1826, in South Salem, where LaGrange street now is. In 1830, he
bought Wyman's Mills, now known as the Forest River Mills, which
were sold to the Forest River Lead Company, in 1843. Mr. Peabody
carried on the lead business until the latter date, and manufactured,
very extensively White Lead, Sheet Lead, and Lead Pipe. About
1833 he built the Paper Mills at Middleton, and made book and print-
ing paper of the very best quality, until he disposed of that property
in 1843. From 1833 to 1837 he sold largely to Gales and Seaton, the
celebrated printers and publishers in Washington. When Mr. Prescott was about commencing the publication of his "History of
Ferdinand and Isabella," the first edition of which was to be brought
out simultaneously in this country and in England, he sent for Mr.
Peabody and showed him his samples of English paper, and was very
desirous to have the American copies equal, if not superior, to the
English, and for that purpose contracted with Mr. Peabody to furnish
him with the paper. The quality of the paper, which Mr. Peabody

manufactured expressly for this work, was very satisfactory to Mr. Prescott, and was considered a very superior article, and probably the best paper which could then have been made in the country. Peabody's paper for blank books was well known among stationers as the best in the market.

About 1836, Mr. Peabody commenced, in South Salem, the business of refining Sperm and Whale Oil, and the manufacture of Sperm Candles. In one year he purchased $100,000 worth of Sperm Oil, and $50,000 worth of Whale Oil. His candles had a great reputation both at home and abroad. He imported the first braiding machine and made the first candles with the braided wick, then considered a great improvement over the common wick. About 1837, Mr. Peabody built Linseed Oil Mills at Middleton, and went largely into the business of making Linseed Oil, importing his flax seed from Europe and from Calcutta. In order to procure larger supplies of seed he chartered, in 1841, the ship General Harrison, and the same year purchased the ship Isaac Hicks, and the next year, the ship New Jersey. These vessels he sent to Calcutta, and they returned to Salem with cargoes of Calcutta goods, and great quantities of Linseed. When the New Jersey arrived in Salem in 1843, it was said that she was the largest merchantman that had ever discharged a cargo here. She registered between 600 and 700 tons, and was a great carrier. The Linseed Oil, like all the other articles manufactured by Mr. Peabody, was of the best quality. At that time there was only one other Linseed Mill in this part of the country, namely, that belonging to Mr. Stearns, at Medford.

Mr. Peabody also shipped to London large quantities of Linseed Cake, used extensively in England for feeding cattle. From this statement it will be seen that Mr. Peabody at one time carried on the following branches of business, namely, White Lead, Sheet Lead, Lead Pipe, Linseed Oil, Sperm and Whale Oil, Sperm Candles and Paper, employing directly and indirectly a great number of men. There were at one time commission houses in New York and Boston employed almost exclusively with his business. The well known firm of Chandler and Howard, in Boston, may be mentioned as an instance. To do the same amount of business Mr. Peabody did when he was manufacturing largely, would now probably involve a capital of over a million of dollars."

Colonel Peabody's manufacturing and commercial operations in Linseed, described by Mr. Brooks, led him to pay particular attention to flax, especially a valuable species of it, grown in Bengal. The plant there reaches a considerable height, and its bark yields the finest and longest strands. The lower part, or but-end, is quite thick, the bark rough, containing irregular threads, of a very short staple. Regarded by the natives as a refuse portion of the shrub, it can be obtained of them at a very low price. He procured some of these but-ends, and went to work upon them in a building erected for the purpose at Kernwood, until he had matured the requisite machinery to disengage and straighten out the fibres, and twist and weld them into continuous threads ; and finally succeeded in producing, out of them, cotton bagging of a superior quality. His factory for this purpose, and the first of the kind ever contrived, recently established here on a large scale, gives employment to a great number of persons. The article wrought in it is called Jute, from the name of the district in Bengal (Chotee) from which the raw material is obtained.

His enterprise and liberality, stimulated by the lively interest he felt in our local annals and antiquities, and his reverence for the memory of the first settlers of this place, took effect in one great service, never to be forgotten, in the historical department of the Essex Institute. It is a matter of record that, in 1670, the Meeting-house of the First Church was superseded by a new one, and that the old building, consisting of two parts, one erected in 1634, the other an enlargement,made in 1639, was thereafter used for various purposes, and ultimately removed from its original site. Tradition, supported by a strong array of certificates from certain individuals who had enjoyed favorable opportunities of receiving information on the subject, and which had long been current, pointed to a building owned by Mr. David Nichols, standing on his premises, in the rear of the tanneries, under the brow of Witch Hill, as the original part of the primitive Meeting-house—that erected in 1634. It was· precisely of the same length, breadth, and height, consisting of a single room, with plastered walls and ceiling, and a garret. It had been used for some time as a lumber-room, but was in a state of decay that would not long have allowed of its being serviceable even in that way. The story was, that at an early period it had been occupied as a wayfarer's inn, a stopping place on the original road from Salem to Lynn; also the only one then travelled between the interior and Marblehead. If it was the veritable Meeting-house, it had, as we know, been used, still earlier in its intermediate history, as a school house. The subject was investigated by the Essex Institute. Mr. Nichols presented the building, and the Salem Athenæum gave a site for it, where it now stands, in the rear of Plummer Hall. Colonel Peabody, who, with the late George A. Ward, had taken a leading interest in the matter, offered to assume the entire expense of the operation of removal and reconstruction. He proceeded, with careful workmen, to direct and superintend the process of taking it to pieces. It was certain from expressions in the record, that, when used as a Meeting-house, there was a gallery at one end, of which, however, at this time, there was no appearance, in the aspect of the room. This circumstance had introduced some perplexity and thrown doubt over the whole subject. There were, however, two upright posts, of great size, equal to that of the corner or main posts, standing opposite to each other, about one third of the distance from one end of the building, and an equally large transverse beam resting on their tops. Why these posts, and the beam above the ceiling connecting them, were placed at one-third instead of one-half the distance in the length of the building, was the question. At first it was thought to favor the supposition that there had been a gallery, which would have confirmed the tradition; for no other use than that of a Meeting-house would have required, or allowed of, a gallery. But there was not height enough, under the rafters, and above the transverse beam, resting as it did on the top of the upright posts and the plate of the frame; and this seemed to negative the idea that the transverse beam was designed to support a gallery. The upright posts had been coated over with some sort of mortar and whitewashed. Upon breaking and picking it off, the original mortices were revealed a few feet below the ceiling, exactly of the size to receive the tenons of the transverse beam, with a shoulder in the upright post at the same point, so that the bearing should be not only upon the tenons, but upon the body of the posts and beam. In knocking away the plaster from the plate, or transverse beam, at the nearest end of the building, grooves were found fitted to receive the upper ends of the joists upon which the floor of the gallery was laid. It seems that when the building was converted to the use of a school room, or when used for any other purpose, the gallery, being found an obstruction and incumbrance, was put out of the way, by raising the front beam on which it rested up to the top of the posts, and a clear ceiling spread under it. No discovery in astronomy, electricity, or other field of science, or search of antiquarian, was ever received with more enthusiastic gratification, than filled the minds of all engaged in the work when these mortices and grooves were brought to light. So much as was undecayed of the timbers and rafters,

side, or consolidated into a grand scheme of knowledge, combining the highest classic titles ever given to seats of learning, the "Peabody Academy of Science and the Essex Institute of Natural and Civil History," will make this another Athens. The fact that one man, our lamented President, was, at the head of both the Academy and the Institute, foreshadows this happy consummation.

Colonel Peabody had strong family and domestic affections. The death of a beloved daughter, on the 12th of December, 1866, produced a shock from which he never recovered. She was worthy of the love and admiration with which all who knew regarded her, and was endeared to her father by earnest and active sympathy in his favorite pursuits, and by embellishments given to his works by her refined taste, and delicate pencil. She died away from home; and the intelligence came unexpectedly upon him. Although he bore it with manly firmness, and the devout submission of a christian, it could not fail to be noticed that his spirit never fully rose again to its accustomed buoyancy. The blow reached the vital centre of his being, and the effect on his general health soon became quite manifest. It was followed, on the 20th of January, 1867, with a slight apoplectic attack, which was repeated on the 2d of September.

After the death of his daughter I had a long conversation with him, in which he laid bare before me the sentiment of his soul under the bereavement; and I can truly say that I have never witnessed a stronger manifestation of the resignation and faith, that are the highest and last attainments of a follower of the Saviour. His spirit bowed in humble but elevated recognition of the Providence that orders and numbers our days, and was sustained by the consolations and reflections that will come, under such an affliction, bringing peace to a believing and thoughtful mind.

About the time of the announcement of the donation by his friend and kinsman for the advancement of science among us, in developing some of his views as to its proper application, he expressed to me the expectation that he should not live long, and might at any moment be taken away. He spoke on the subject with perfect calmness, and in a manner to convince me that his thoughts and views had been brought to a state of perparation for the summons whenever it should come. He entered particularly upon the consideration of such an event in connection with his plans as charged with the trust of organizing the Academy in accordance with the purposes, and fulfilment of the wishes, of its illustrious founder. This led to general remarks on the subject of death, especially if it should suddenly come, and he expressed the idea, that he felt no anxiety, and allowed himself to indulge no preferences, as to the time or mode of its occurrence, but experienced entire relief in leaving all to a Providence that was infinitely wise and benignant. I was much impressed with the seriousness, sincerity, perfect acquiescence of spirit, and devout submission to the Divine will, he manifested throughout. His instincts were religious, and had ever been cherished by reflection, and strengthened by habit. The sentiments he expressed were evidently such as he had long entertained, of the willingness and readiness, with which every child of God ought to-commit life and events to the disposal of The Father.

During the month of October he continued to fail. On the afternoon of the 29th, when standing at the window of his chamber, looking out upon the cold and blustering

10

autumnal air, and following the foliage, falling from the branches that had sustained its life, blown hither and thither, and strown on the ground, he said, "we do all fade as a leaf," and immediately turned to his bed. He fell, at once, into a quiet and gentle sleep from which he never awoke in the body. Not a pang, nor a struggle, nor a movement, told when his spirit passed away. His death, only indicated by his ceasing to breathe, was in the evening of the 31st of October, 1867.

In looking over the memoir that has now been presented, justice requires me again to state, that it is but a cursory and quite imperfect enumeration of the scientific and mechanical operations in which the life of Francis Peabody was employed. Fully described, they would require a minute technical analysis such as only persons particularly conversant with such subjects could present; and ranging, as they do, over so many distinct departments, demand separate treatises. In the course of the narrative many traits of his character have incidentally been given. Some general views of it may properly be offered in conclusion.

Colonel Peabody was a business man of marked energy, exactitude and capacity. As a manufacturer and merchant his transactions showed sagacity, prudence, and intelligence. Like all his other engagements, they were suggested and guided by his predominating taste for scientific pursuits, and the knowledge thus acquired. His business operations were illustrations, on a large scale, of the application of philosophy to practical objects. His experiments and studies were, in one sense, kept in subordination to his business, and never allowed to occupy his time or engross his thoughts, to the disadvantage of any important interests in which he was

concerned. Although all but profuse in the expenditure
of money in the prosecution of investigations, he was
never wasteful, inconsiderate, or careless in its use. He
exercised his own judgment in the application of his
means, made his outlays in such directions as he saw fit,
and could not easily be drawn upon by inducements, addressed to the love of applause or popularity. His own
idea of the methods in which he could best promote the
public welfare ruled his conduct. In concluding a bar-
gain or a purchase of any kind, he was not to be imposed
upon, and, in no degree, did his enthusiasm in favorite
pursuits detract from his vigilance or caution as a business man. He was as thorough, skilful and extensive a
merchant, as if commerce had been his only employment.
For some years before his death he managed a trade, and
owned a tonnage, equal to that of his father, when the
ships of that great merchant frequented every port of the
Altantic shore of Europe from the Baltic to Gibralter,
around the Mediterranean, and in both the Indies. And
what was most extraordinary, with all his ships, cargoes,
manufactures, building houses, embellishing estates, experiments in the laboratory, operations in the workshop,
and the study of authorities from the shelves and cases of
his library, he was, as much as any man among us, on
hand to participate in local interests or social movements,
ready to attend to any call for consultation or coöperation, and apparently at leisure to enjoy intercourse, or
engage in conversation, with any one at any time. Always busy, but never in such a hurry that he could not
stop to converse with friends or townsmen, as met by the
way—with time to spare for all the demands of family,
neighborhood, or society. The activity and elasticity of
his faculties never failed. His inexhaustible spirits sup-

plied both mind and body with inexhaustible strength. He was never known to be tired, and did not seem to need rest. His business and his amusements were so organized that they never interfered with each other. His multifarious engagements were so methodized that he could, whenever he chose, fly away from them; but present or absent, his business went on, his vessels kept under sail, and the wheels of his mills continued to revolve. Few men have done more work, and few have found more gratification outside of what is ordinarily called work. In this respect he was remarkably successful in solving the problem of life. He experienced an equal exhilaration, in meeting its obligations and enjoying its pleasures. He turned its labors into pleasures, and kept the heart in sunshine however dark the cloud over head.

He must be allowed to have been one of the most useful persons we have ever had among us. The period of his activity in the affairs of society embraced nearly half a century, and, from first to last, he spread activity around him. The various industrial enterprises he started, the institutions of usefulness he helped to establish, and the numbers he brought into employment in several departments of business and labor, constitute an aggregate scarcely to be estimated, and not often to be traced to one originating mind. At the time of his death, and for many years before, it is probable that, at least three hundred persons were profitably occupied in carrying on his business by sea and by land, in trades, arts, labors, and handicraft of all sorts. And it is observable that the employments he thus opened will continue to diffuse their benefits and privileges to countless numbers indefinitely; for experience has shown that his enterprises were the result of good judgment and stand the test of time. The machines he improved and constructed, the processes he introduced, the manufactures he set in motion, lead works, paper oil and jute mills, some of them passed into other hands, are still, and probably always will be, in vigorous and prosperous action. The buildings he erected or embellished, the lecture-room he designed, like his stone arch at Harmony Grove, have durability impressed on them, survive their constructor, and bid fair to survive the lapse of generations.

He was a good citizen in all respects, regarding with interest the advancement of society, and retaining to the end a disposition to aid in all enterprises that commended themselves to his judgment. While always ready to act with others, he was often in a minority upon local as well as national questions, but he loved the people and rejoiced in their prosperity and happiness. He was a true patriot. Nothing could wean him from attachment and devotion to his country. No extent of what he might have thought mal-administration : no defeat of the parties to which he may have belonged, whether based upon questions of policy affecting the general government of the Union, or on state or municipal affairs ; no amount of supposed error or wrong in the temporary phases of society ; none of the trappings of foreign courts or seductions of foreign travel; neither the pomp nor pageantry elsewhere seen, nor the glitter which wealth, like his, in other forms of society enables its possessor to command, could estrange him from the land of his birth or the home of his fathers. While abroad he gloried in and yearned for his country, and came back, each time, with a conviction that there was no country like his own, and no spot, in that country, better than this to live in, and die in. His conviction that our institutions are

founded in truth and right, and his faith in their perpe-
tuity, were never shaken, and his vision of the future
glories of America never grew dim.

Few men have been more free from pride or pretension,
in spirit or manners. The riches he had inherited and
accumulated, did not lift him out of the community, or
estrange him from the sentiments, ways, or company of
the common people. He talked and acted with them as
an equal. To this admirable trait of his character a
cloud of witnesses could be raised from every position in
society, and in every stage of his life. Such a man was
a true republican, to whatever party he belonged.

His private character, from the beginning to the end of
life, was irreproachable. No taint ever sullied the purity
of his sentiments. Neither fashion nor folly undermined
the integrity of his principles. He was a temperate,
exemplary, ingenuous, and honest man. The utterances
of his lips, as well as the habits of his life, were always
under the restraints of propriety. He respected all that
was excellent, and reverenced all that is sacred in
humanity. His thoughts were innocent, his affections
kind, and his faith in man and in God immovable. He
appreciated the value of religious institutions, and re-
posed, with steadfast fidelity, on his religious convictions.
He allowed no vain speculations or casual annoyances, to
cast a shadow on the path that leads the christian heart to
the service and worship of God.

The example, that has now been contemplated, presents
a moral, which I would leave particularly impressed on
every mind.

"The vanity of human wishes" is not the morbid com-
plaint of a melancholy temperament. It is a solemn
verity. Failure to realize mere worldly happiness is the

lesson taught by universal experience. The fact that this lesson is never received, is the mystery and enigma of life. We toil and struggle with ever unabated eagerness for what, upon clutching it, always proves an illusion. We find it to be a shadow but pursue it still. To an eye, looking down upon the sublunary scene, what a strange spectacle is presented in the whole race of man absorbed in this always baffled effort, this never ceasing, ever fruitless chase. Wealth, it is thought certain, will place in our hands the embellishments and blessings of life, and secure perpetual contentment. We gain it; but elegant mansions and overflowing incomes, leave the soul poorer than before. Existence, desire accomplished, becomes a burden; and we sink into dreary dulness, or fly to other abodes, which in turn soon grow wearisome; again we shift the scene, and wander without rest and without a home. Ambition contends for the prizes of public station. They may all be won, and the successful aspirant left the most dissatisfied citizen of the state. The young king of Macedon sighed for universal dominion; and entered upon a career to attain it, crowded with more success than ever reached before or since; but at its close, when the whole world, subjected to his victorious arms, was at his feet, wept for other worlds to conquer. The Hebrew monarch surveyed his riches and splendors and luxuries and glories, and revealed to himself the utter emptiness of them all—"vanity of vanities—all is vanity." The history of the ages confirms the teachings of our own observation and experience, and stamps disappointment upon the fulfilment of earthly hopes.

When Francis Peabody had reached the age of manhood and become the head of a household, he was in possession of all the happiness that can be desired or imagined, and it lasted through life. Why this exemption from the lot of humanity? Because his faculties and aspirations had early opened and entered upon a field, outside of, and above, the sphere in which enjoyment is ordinarily sought. In the pursuit of knowledge, in forms that included the ever exhilarating activities of the intellect, he found the elixir whose infusion in his cup kept it from palling on his lips.

Let every young man, especially let those in the possession or the acquisition of fortune, secure a like refuge, by choosing some department of science, philosophy, literature, or art, and make it a recreation amidst the toils of business, and a refreshment when other objects lose their zest. He who adopts this course, will have, ever after, no void in his heart, no weariness in his hours. His labors will all be lightened, his joys will retain their relish, contentment and cheerfulness will crown his days. The elasticity of his spirits, and the enthusiasm of his youth, will continue unimpaired to the end.

The foregoing Memoir was read at a meeting of the Essex Institute, July 18, 1868, the President, Dr. Henry Wheatland, in the chair. At its conclusion, Hon. Asahel Huntington, Ex-President of the Society, after speaking in strong terms of praise of the reader's treatment of his theme, offered the following vote, which, being seconded by Abner C. Goodell, Jr., Esq., Vice-President, was unanimously passed:

"That the thanks of the Institute be presented to Mr. Upham for his address, and that the same be referred to the appropriate Committee for publication."

www.ingramcontent.com/pod-product-compliance
Lightning Source LLC
Chambersburg PA
CBHW022143090426
42742CB00010B/1369